READING EASY 1800-50

Published Sep.10th 1821 by LONGMAN HURST & Co Paternoster Row

G. S. Chalmers

READING EASY 1800-50

*A study of the teaching of reading
with a list of the books which were used
and a selection of facsimile pages.*

London

The Broadsheet King

To Karen

ISBN 0 902617 16 8

Photo-typeset in Century Textbook by Speedimage Ltd.,
Worthing.

The Broadsheet King,
15 Mortimore Terrace, London, N.W.5

ACKNOWLEDGEMENTS

I am indebted to Professor G. H. Bantock who read this study while it was in preparation and made many helpful suggestions; to the staff of the Technical Library, Corby, the Branch Library, Corby, and the School of Education Library, Leicester; to Mrs Anne Renier; and especially to Gerald and Doris Coe, whose knowledge of antiquarian books helped me greatly in the compilation of Appendix A.

The quotations from *In Spite of the Alphabet* appear by permission of Messrs. Chatto & Windus and the late Hunter Diack.

CONTENTS

FOREWORD

There are few books available which attempt to set out the history and analyse the contents of books used in England for the teaching of reading. Hunter Diack in his study of the teaching of reading, *In Spite of the Alphabet*,[1] pointed out the difficulties, and went some way towards solving them. Many of the problems are problems of terminology, and many of the differences between methods, differences in terminology. These differences led Diack to stress that each of the methods 'is amoebic in its power to change shape.'[2] For the purpose of this study I have used as a basis the classification used in the report *The Teaching of Reading* discussed at the 12th. International Conference on Education, 1949, which was used by W.S. Gray in his survey *The Teaching of Reading and Writing*.[3]

Early methods of teaching reading fall into two groups — the synthetic and the analytic. Synthetic methods were the earliest to be used; they lay stress on the elements of words — the letters or syllables. When the elements have been learned they can be combined into larger units — words and phrases. In the spelling method, the names of letters are used in order to recognize and pronounce words. In simple phonic methods, the sounds of the letters are used. In more advanced phonic methods, the sounds of digraphs are added, and some attempt is made to deal with the final e in words such as mite, mute, mate, mote, by teaching a-e, i-e, o-e, u-e, as phonograms. The syllabic methods follow naturally on either spelling or phonic methods. Since many consonants can only be pronounced correctly when combined with vowels, a syllabic method can be used as a starting-point in teaching reading, the vowels being introduced first. Phonetic methods make use of diacritical marks or changes of spelling; a spelling or phonic attack can then be used by the pupil.

Analytic methods use meaningful language units as a starting-point. The meaning of what is to be read is emphasized from the start. Word methods are based on the assumption that each word has a characteristic shape by which it can be remembered. Later the pupil's attention is directed to the details — the syllables, letters and sounds — so that he may be able to attack new, unknown words. In the phrase method it is assumed that phrases are more interesting to the pupil than words. In the sentence method, the sentence is regarded as the true unit of language.

The names 'Alphabetic' or 'ABC method' can be misleading. An alphabetic method can be either a spelling or a phonic method. In books and reports written during the period under review, alphabetic methods may be condemned and a simple phonic method recommended, or a word method may be advocated where an alphabetic method, which we know to have been phonic, has been in use.

A further complication can arise when methods are combined — a teacher may start by naming the letter and teaching its sound immediately afterwards.[4] On other occasions, instead of combining methods, a teacher may appear to be using half-methods. Teachers who used word methods frequently taught recognition of words by shape, but failed at later stages to direct the pupils' attention to details. Furthermore, even when we can establish which books were in use in certain schools, there is no guarantee that teachers used the material in the expected way. The authors of some early 'Spellers' were aware of this and took pains to point out that they could not give advice on methods of teaching reading. A spelling book, designed for use with a spelling method, may have been used as a basis for a word method of teaching.

'Often writers on this subject use the term "method" when it would have been more logical to refer to "teaching material" as, for example, when a teacher is said to be using "the phonic method" when she is in fact teaching by an alphabetic method though using books designed for teaching by a phonic method.[5]

Finally, when we have established which methods were in use, it is always possible that the children learned to read by methods of their own. After chanting many tedious tables of syllables, a child with a good visual memory may have found it easier to learn the words which followed as wholes, and may have become a proficient reader using a word method, while others in the class were laboriously joining up syllables.

Foreword

NOTES
1. Hunter Diack, *In Spite of the Alphabet*, Chatto & Windus, 1965.
2. *Ibid.*, p.7
3. W.S. Gray, *The Teaching of Reading and Writing*, U.N.E.S.C.O., 1963
4. Diack, *op. cit.*, p.21
5. *Ibid.*, p.8

PART 1.

THE EIGHTEENTH CENTURY BACKGROUND

The eighteenth century, which saw great changes in attitude towards education and children, has been described as the 'Age of Benevolence' for philanthropic and religious work. Education was important to anyone concerned with such work. At the beginning of the century, children were regarded as miniature adults; Comenius's views on primary education had been largely disregarded; his *Orbis Pictus*, the first picture book for children, was probably the only one that made concessions to childhood. A more typical example of the few children's books that existed was Janeway's *A Token for Children* (1671), which was 'an account of the conversion, holy and exemplary lives, and joyful deaths of several young children.' In the second half of the century, under the influence of Locke and Rousseau, attempts were made to produce schoolbooks which would appeal to the child's interests, written in language that the child could understand.

The traditional way of learning to read was to master the Criss-Cross Row, or Hornbook, a sheet of paper mounted on a board and covered with horn. A simple hornbook had a cross in the top left-hand corner, the alphabet in roman letter, black letter and italic. The alphabet was taught by pointing to the letters in turn and asking the child to name them. No attempt was made at this stage to teach the sounds of the letters. The alphabet was followed by the vowels, double letters and various punctuation marks. The sounds of the vowels were learned in order to master the syllabarium which followed — so this was not a pure spelling method; some knowledge of phonics was introduced, as Hunter Diack has pointed out.[1] Nevertheless, the syllables were taught by naming the letters: ay, bee, ab - ee, bee, eb. The number of syllables presented to the child was small:

ab	eb	ib	ob	ub		ba	be	bi	bo	bu
ac	ec	ic	oc	uc		ca	ce	ci	co	cu
ad	ed	id	od	ud		da	de	di	do	du

The child spelled the syllabarium through backwards and forwards, down, up and across until every one of the meaningless syllables was lodged firmly in his memory. Last of all in the hornbook was the Lord's Prayer, which was spelled out word by word and read aloud. The child was then ready to spell out the words in the Bible.

This method had remained basically unchanged since the ninth century. Similar methods were in use in Greece in 350 B.C. How effective a method it was is uncertain. Diack argued that:

Alphabetic methods have the peculiar distinction of not having been shown by some manipulation of statistics to be inferior to all other methods or combination of methods. . . . Since no method has been shown to *everybody's* satisfaction to be superior to all other methods, there does not seem to be complete justification for regarding alphabetic methods as inherently inefficient.[2]

The Spelling method was suited to black letter; in the Middle Ages reading was necessarily reading aloud.[3] Even proficient readers of black letter might have difficulty in recognizing the words as wholes, and would have to decipher a word letter by letter. This country had been late in adopting roman type for vernacular use; the turning point had come in 1612 with the reissue of Barker's Bible in roman characters, but black letter was still in use in chapbooks in the first half of the eighteenth century. No doubt, when he had finished his hornbook and had practised spelling out words, a child would come to recognize them as wholes in roman characters, or would deduce the sounds of the letters in order to have a method of attack on unknown words. Reading for meaning would be discouraged by this method, particularly if the difficult vocabulary of the Bible was all the child could practise on.

The compilers of spelling books of the early eighteenth century, such as Markham, Dyche and Dixon, used the hornbook as a basis for their books. They began with the alphabet and lists of syllables to be spelled out. There was a growing awareness, however, of the importance of the sounds of the letters. The syllabic method was added naturally as the obvious way of building upon a knowledge of the 'powers' of the letters. The second part of Thomas Dyche's *Guide to the English Tongue* (1707), 'for some as are advanced to some ripeness of judgement', contained 'observations of the sounds of letters and dipthongs; rules for the true division of syllables'. An appendix contained 'many additional lessons in prose and verse; first in words of one syllable only; and then mixed with words of two, three, four, five, six and seven syllables.'

These spelling books were meant to be used by parents and private tutors, and their influence was considerable. The combination of spelling, simple phonic and syllabic methods persisted throughout the following century, and into this. Dyche was printed many times in the eighteenth century, and again in 1811. Dixon's *English Instructor* (1728) reached its 68th. edition in 1822; Markham's *Introduction to Spelling and Reading English* (c. 1720) was still listed by Routledge in 1860.

The importance of home teaching must be stressed; most teaching of reading in the eighteenth century was done in the home. The growth of the Charity School movement encouraged this trend; the pioneers of the S.P.C.K. offered elementary education to 'all girls who cared to come forward', as well as to boys. In December, 1717, a Mr. Barrington of Shrivenham wrote:

The first regard would be more properly bestowed on the girls because the care of families (in the country especially) falls under the direction of the mother.[4]

The education of girls must have had a considerable effect on the level of literacy by the end of the century, accounting in part for the increased printing of alphabet books and battledores after 1750, although the poorest mothers would have made their own. Unfortunately, little attention was paid to material of this sort in the past, and few home-made books have survived. A few may be seen in the Edinburgh Corporation Museum of Childhood.

The motives in establishing Charity Schools were varied. Many philanthropists could see no way of distributing wealth equally, but saw education as a way of making life less brutish for the poor.[5] The middle classes tended to accept social inequality as God's will; they believed that education would ensure social discipline,[6] improve morals and make better servants, as can be seen in the regular apologies for educating the poor that preachers made at the Annual Service. Little attention was given to the greater happiness that education could bring.

This outlook was reflected in the handbook for Charity School teachers, which was Dr. James Talbot's *Christian Schoolmaster* (1707). Talbot regarded the mind of a child as a blank paper on which a teacher could imprint the 'fundamental duties of our Holy Religion'. Charity Schools taught industry; reading was taught on the grounds that it was a good basis for religious training. The skill of the craftsman, the traditional culture and religion were all that were felt to be necessary. For most of the century the text-book in use was the Bible, usually bound with the Prayer Book. Children were not to be taught anything 'to set them above the condition of servants, or the more laborious employments.' Away from London, good teachers were difficult to obtain. One or two seem to have been outstanding — Sims of Cripplegate, known as 'the Father of Charity Schoolmasters', announced in 1707 a method of teaching the alphabet in one day. Agents of the S.P.C.K. reported favourably, and many managers of country schools sent young men to Sims for training. Unfortunately, no record of his method has survived. After the first wave of enthusiasm, and partly as a result of the failure of the Schools of Industry, Charity Schools declined until the end of the century. The education they provided was usually better than that of the Dame Schools. The hours of attendance were seven to eleven o'clock and one to five o'clock in summer, beginning an hour later and ending an hour earlier in winter, with five weeks holiday a year. School began and ended with a prayer, and Church attendance was compulsory on Sundays; sometimes on Wednesdays and Fridays as well. Children attended between the ages of four and eleven, or even older. There were usually four classes: the first was the elementary reading class; in the second, children were taught to read the New Testament and Psalms; in the third, the whole Bible, and to write; in the fourth, the four rules of number were taught if necessary to boys who were to be apprenticed. The catechism was taught continually. When enough children could say it, notice was given to the minister who would examine them publicly in Church. There were frequent 'Open Days' when benefactors and trustees would hear the children's answers.[7] At the beginning of the next century, Mrs. Trimmer's *Teacher's Assistant* had replaced *The Christian Schoolmaster*. Mrs. Trimmer stressed that Charity schoolchildren should be made to feel grateful and meek. However, she was much less precise on methods of teaching reading. The alphabet was taught by the spelling method. The 'true spelling of words and the use of stops' was important. The reading book was the Anglican catechism.

Portions that had not already been memorised were chosen so that 'by frequent repetition of words, while they are thus practising to read them, they may become familiar both to their eyes and memory.' This was not an analytic method stressing the meaning of words from the start, but a synthetic method, which involved wearisome drill in the alphabet and the breaking down of words into syllables and letters as an aid to word recognition. Next came the Book of Common Prayer, the Psalms of David in the Prayer Book version, the New Testament and the Old Testament. Writing was introduced only when children could read 'competently well'.

By the end of the eighteenth century, attitudes to education and children had changed; although Locke's views on the nature of personality put forward in his *Essay Concerning Human Understanding* (1690-1706) and *Some Thoughts Concerning Education* (1699) — for instance, that a child's mind was a clean sheet ready to be written upon — were in evidence in *The Christian Schoolmaster*. Rousseau, in *Emile* (1762) stressed the growing mind, reacted against imposing ideas on a child — and organized his protest into a scheme of education. *Emile* was available in translation in 1763, but its impact was strengthened by the arrival of the French emigres after the Revolution. Isaac Watts' *Divine Songs, attempted in easy language, for the use of children* (1715) was perhaps the first true children's book, an honour usually given to John Newbery's *A Little Pretty Pocket Book; intended for the Instruction and Amusement of Little Master Tommy, and Pretty Miss Polly*, (1744), which was sold with a ball and a pin-cushion. Newbery was perhaps the first to unite 'Instruction and Amusement'. The book was followed by a steady stream for middle-class children, who were delighted by something more entertaining than *Pilgrim's Progress*.

Schoolbooks remained largely unaffected by this new outlook for some time. The first manifestations occurred at the pre-reading stage. Nursery rhymes to teach the alphabet were already in print in chapbook form; *The Tragical Death of A, Apple-Pye* was well-known to children; *A was an Archer* appeared in a mixture of roman and black letter ca. 1703. From 1750, however, printed alphabet sheets, which had originated before the hornbook, took on a more attractive form. From 1770 onwards, hornbooks were superseded by battledores, which were becoming very popular. They were little three-leaved cards with attractive covers that could be folded into an oblong shape with a flap left over to form a handle. They contained alphabets, numerals, easy reading lessons and little wood-cuts. The reading lessons sometimes took the form of moral tales, but religious teaching was avoided. Hornbooks with wooden handles had been used by children as bats or racquets; the name Battledore was used to encourage this. Collins of Salisbury, an associate of Newbery, first listed the *Royal Battledore* in 1750; in 1770 it was the first part of Newbery's *Circle of the Sciences*. Between 1771 and 1780 Collins sold 100,000 battledores at a penny each.

After 1778, simple readers appeared which were more suitable for the nursery than the badly-printed chapbooks or the output of the Newbery press, in which the primary aim was amusement. Mrs. Barbauld's *Lessons for Children, from two to three years old* was issued in that year. The author had been unable to find a book adapted to the comprehension of little children, printed on good paper, in large type, with wide spaces between the lines. Criticised by the Edgeworths, it was modified and became extremely popular, remaining in print after 1850. Mrs. Trimmer welcomed it as giving 'a new turn to the composition and mode of printing books for little children', and was inspired to produce her *Little Spelling Book for Young Children* (1786), later known as *The Charity School Spelling Book*. Lady Fenn's graded reading primers had appeared in 1783; *Cobwebs to Catch Flies*; or, Dialogues in short sentences, adapted to children, from the age of three to eight years. . . .Vol. 1 containing easy lessons in words of three letters, four letters, five letters, six letters suited to children from three to five years of age. . . .Vol. 2 containing instructive lessons in words of one syllable, two syllables, three syllables, four syllables, suited to children from five to eight years.

Cobwebs to Catch Flies was meant to amuse as much as to instruct; but again the books were printed in large type, with wide spaces between the lines. They were still in print in 1867. In *A Spelling Book, designed to render the Rudiments of our native language easy and pleasant* (c. 1790), Lady Fenn included a catalogue of books 'recommended to children from the age of three to twelve years'. Most of the books were published by John Marshall, Lady Fenn's publisher, and included primers of all kinds — Universal, Silver, Rational, Picturesque — and progressive readers which began with stories in words of one syllable, although there was sometimes some cheating with hyphens.

The growing interest in children's readers was matched by an increase in the number of spelling books, spelling dictionaries, and 'Reading Easy' books, the compilers of which made brave attempts to graft Amusement on to Instruction, hoping that they would appeal to parents as well as to schools. Paley's book, *The Young Christian Instructed in Reading* (1790), was later issued as *Reading Made Completely Easy, or,*

A necessary introduction to reading the Bible: consisting chiefly of Scripture sentences: each lesson of which is disposed in such order, as the learner is led on with pleasure, step by step, from simple and easy, to compound and difficult words: which is allowed by all to be the most regular, speedy and rational method of teaching. Recommended for the use of schools.

It contained also 'The Trifler, or Pretty Plaything' and 'Tom Thumb's Alphabet', with four full-page cuts and ninety-four small cuts. Masson's *English Spelling Book* was reissued in 1794 with a collection of fables added. Hastie's *Only Method to Make Reading Easy* (c. 1782) had twenty-four miniature cuts by Thomas Bewick to illustrate animals, birds, and the letters of the alphabet. Most of the Reading Easy books followed the same pattern, even *The Real Reading Made Easy* (1782), an imitation of Hastie's *Only Method*, also with cuts by Bewick, which was propaganda for simplified spelling, and contained 'A Su'pl'int To Thi Histire ov Robinsin Kruzo'. Many were published for local schoolmasters by small printing firms, probably in very small editions. The title pages were worded in a similar way:

An introduction to reading the Holy Bible: consisting of Scripture and moral lessons, so disposed that the learner is led on with pleasure, step by step, from simple to easy, to compound and difficult words; which is allowed by all to be the most regular, speedy, and rational way of teaching. (Davies, T., *The Newest Reading Made Completely Easy.*)

Tom Thumb's Alphabet, A was an Archer, or a fable and a few cuts were added, together with 'recommended for the use of schools'. The titles of a number of these books will be found in Appendix A.

Two of the spelling books were well-known in America: Dilworth's *New Guide to the English Tongue* (1740) and Fenning's *Universal Spelling Book* (1756), which was still listed by Routledge in 1860, and deserves closer attention.

The alphabet is presented in a way similar to that of the hornbook, with an enlarged syllabarium:

ba	be	bi	bo	bu		ab	eb	ib	ob	ub
ca	ce	ci	co	cu		ac	ec	ic	oc	uc
da	de	di	do	du		ad	ed	id	od	ud
fa	fe	fi	fo	fu		af	ef	if	of	uf
ka	ke	ki	ko	ku		ak	ek	ik	ok	uk
la	le	li	lo	lu		al	el	il	ol	ul
ma	me	mi	mo	mu		am	em	im	om	um
na	ne	ni	no	nu		an	en	in	on	un

Let the child be taught to pronounce ce the same as se and ci the same as si.

Lessons 3 and 4 are tables of double or treble consonants in front of vowels:

bla	ble	bli	blo	blu		bra	bre	bri	bro	bru
cla	cle	cli	clo	clu		cra	cre	cri	cro	cru
pla	ple	pli	plo	plu		pra	pre	pri	pro	pru
sla	sle	sli	slo	slu		tra	tre	tri	tro	tru
fra	fre	fri	fro	fru		phra	phre	phri	phro	phru

Lesson 5 contains 'Proper words of one syllable, both natural and easy to spell and read.'

All am and are be he me we the thee ye by my thy do go nor not of off from on or so to too two up us you

This is a step towards the spelling books of the next century which gave common words, usually of one syllable, 'to be known at sight.' This was still not the 'word' method of teaching reading: the words had to be learned before reading began.

Tables 6 to 14 contained

words from two to four syllables, and lessons, from where the syllables are undivided for trial, which are both easy and instructive; and though not so many in number as in some books, yet they are enow for common instruction, to qualify any school-boy to read with practice.

Tables 15 and 16 contained fables and useful stories,

not only improving to the mind and morals, but which will greatly conduce to help children to read well.

Tables 17, 18, 19 dealt with homonyms, contractions, and the use of numbers.

Tables 20 to 23

treat of words spelt alike, but pronounced differently; as also of the names and use of all the stops and marks in reading and writing.

Later sections of the book contain a Guide to English Grammar; a collection of 5000 words arranged syllabically; many useful things. . .with a variety of Alphabetical copies and writing-pieces; Chronological Tables. . .also the alphabet in small and great letters of the Old English Print.

Fenning must have been aware of criticisms of dullness in the syllabic method of teaching. In the 1767 preface he points out that

a perpetual jargon of ace, brace, grace, trace; buy, dry, fry, shy, fly, &c. &c. is dull, dry and tiresome, both to the child and his teacher; and especially as there are many masters and mistresses so ignorant (particularly in small towns) as to think it really necessary to go through all the words in every table; though they contain many thousands.

A move towards analytic methods is indicated by the next comment:

It is more natural for little boys and girls to like the sound of cake, pie, tart, top, bread, beer, cup, dish, spoon, plate, knife, fork, &c. which, though they may seem hard, yet really are not so: because they know the names, and having an idea of the things before-hand, they are half-taught.

Unfortunately, the child still had to learn these interesting words before he was allowed to read.

The success of a spelling-book seems to have depended less on the method of teaching reading which it advocated than on its possible use as an all purpose text-book. Fisher's *Instructor* (c. 1731) went further than most; it contained spelling, reading, writing and arithmetic. Later editions had added to them The Family's Companion, a compendium of the sciences of geography and astronomy.

In this country no book dominated education as did the *New-England Primer* or Noah Webster's *Spelling Book* in America. However, the *Royal Primer* (Newbery and Collins c. 1750) was much influenced by the *New-England Primer* and remained popular into the nineteenth century.

Although the sounds of the vowels were taught as a preliminary to syllabic methods, there does not seem to have been any further progress towards a phonic method in this country apart from the work of a teacher in Newcastle whose book was published in 1801, and will be examined in Part 2. An analytic approach was adopted, however, in Thomas

Smith's *Easy Spelling Book, for Children*, in which, although
the material is graded according to the number of syllables in
the words, the word recognition method is used to teach
reading. Comenius, in *Orbis Pictus* (1654) had advocated a
word method; he argued that if words were presented along
with pictures representing their meaning they could be
learned more rapidly, avoiding the 'tedious spelling' which
was a 'troublesome torture of wits'.

Efforts to make learning a diversion led to letters made of
gingerbread, and to David Manson's set of 'Literary Cards'
(1764)

invented for the improvement of children in learning and morals, from their
beginning to learn their letters, till they become proficient in spelling,
reading, parsing, and arithmetic.

In 1770 John Marshall issued *The Art of Teaching in Sport*,
later known as *The Friend of Mothers*;

designed as a prelude to a set of toys, for enabling ladies to instill the
rudiments of spelling, reading, grammar, and arithmetic, under the idea of
amusement.

While these attempts to make learing more palatable
derived from the influence of Locke and Rousseau, so did the
Moral Tale, the direct descendant of Puritan literature.
R.L. Edgeworth and his daughter Maria did much to
popularise and adapt Rousseau's ideas in *Practical
Education* (1798). Maria Edgeworth, Dorothy and Jane
Kilner, Mrs. Barbauld, Mrs. Trimmer, Lady Fenn, Mary
Elliot and Mrs. Sherwood were determined that only the
correct things should be written on the blank mind of the
child. I have not included moral tales in the list of books in
Appendix A unless they have some connection with the
teaching of reading, had a graded vocabulary, or were
adapted to a syllabic method. Moral tales were often used as
first readers when it was realized that the step from the
alphabet and syllabarium to the Bible was too great.
Probably the most popular book for this purpose was written
by a predecessor of the 'monstrous regiment' of women,
Mrs. Ann Slack, who *Pleasing Instructor,* or,

Entertaining Moralist, consisting of select essays, relations, visions, and
allegories from the most eminent English authors,

first printed in 1756, was pirated, and remained popular well
into the nineteenth century.

Moral tales were used by Hannah More in her Cheap Repository Tracts (1795-1798) which were produced to compete with chapbooks. They were 'decked out with rakish titles and woodcuts' and 'sent out, like sheep in wolves' clothing', to be sold by hawkers in competition with their 'old trash'.[8] In 1799 the Religious Tract Society was founded to continue the work.

Hannah More and Mrs. Trimmer were also associated with the Sunday School movement, started by Robert Raikes in 1785. The industrial revolution had brought a large increase in the child population of manufacturing towns. Since the factories were closed on Sundays, schools could open without taking cheap labour from the machines, and teachers would be more readily available. It was rare for a Sunday School to teach more than reading. One of the rules of a York Sunday School stated that

The religious observance of the Christian Sabbath being an essential object with the society, the exercises of the scholars on that day will be restricted to reading in the Old and New Testaments, and to spelling as a preparation for it.[9]

By 1787, 250,000 pupils were in attendance at Sunday Schools,[10] and a spelling book had already been produced for them — *The Salisbury Spelling Book* (Easton, 1786), 'with historical and moral extracts from the New Testament.'

The Industrial Revolution led to the organisation of the pauper as a distinct class; a necessary part of the social order. The philanthropists, in encouraging education, had hoped to improve morals, prevent social disturbances, and make better servants. The results of educating the poor were somewhat different; moreover, after the doctrines of the French Revolution became known, the working classes began to demand greater educational opportunity. Education enabled them to read seditious pamphlets and books against Christianity. Many agreed with Paine that

A nation under a well-regulated government would permit none to remain uninstructed. It is monarchical and aristocratical government that requires ignorance for its support.[11]

It is difficult to estimate how many of the poor were literate at the end of the eighteenth century. The numbers of children in attendance at schools can be misleading; many attended for only a few months; perhaps long enough to master the alphabet and to be able to read chapbooks from the running stationers. They would not have been counted as literate if they could not sign their names, or read the Bible. Judging by the output of the Dicey press and of other chapbook publishers, and by the outstanding success of the Cheap Repository Tracts,[12] many more of the poor could read simple English than has been thought in the past. The Methodists formed a largely literate group; from the time of Wesley, they had issued a wide range of cheap literature; the Methodist class meetings, groups formed for communal devotion, had been meeting also for reading and discussion, and had become an important factor in popular education. The views of James Lackington in his *Memoirs* (1791) have been disputed, but are worth quoting:

The sale of books in general has increased prodigiously within the last twenty years. The poorer sort of farmers, and even the poor country people in general who before that period spent their winter evenings in relating stories of witches, ghosts, hobgoblins etc. now shorten their winter nights by hearing their sons and daughters read tales, romances etc., ... In short, all ranks and degrees now read.[13]

There seems to have been a general increase in reading and publishing in the last quarter of the century. A German schoolmaster who visited the Leipzig Book Fair every year, noted in 1787 that

No other form of literary manufactory is so active as book-making for young people of all grades and classes. . . . . They take all kinds of names and forms: almanacks for children, newspapers for children, journals for children, collections for children, stories for children, comedies for children, dramas for children, geography for children, history for children, physics for children, logic for children, catechisms for children, travels for children, morals for children, grammars for children, and reading books for children in all languages without number, poetry for children, sermons for children, letters for children, talks for children, and unlimited variations on the same theme.[14]

There was an increasing demand for circulating libraries; novels were extremely popular. Working class readers were beginning to tire of the abridged and adulterated tales of chivalry provided by chapbooks, but were reading political tracts. Children were turning from chapbooks, which were often extremely unsuitable, to the books by Newbery and his imitators: reading was becoming an entertainment. That reading was a useful art was another reason put forward for educating the poor, but it was felt that some control should be kept over what was read, either by encouraging the reading of moral tales at the expense of fairy tales and other 'trash', or by suppressing publications that gave the poor 'ideas above their station'. There was a growing feeling that education — particularly the teaching of reading — was necessary for varying reasons. More and more people were learning to read. Who should control education became an arguing point at the beginning of the nineteenth century.

NOTES

1. Hunter Diack, *In Spite of the Alphabet*, p.12
2. *Ibid.*, p.23.
3. Marshall McLuhan, *The Gutenberg Galaxy*, p.82.
4. W.K. Lowther Clarke, *A History of the S.P.C.K.*, p.41.
5. *Ibid.*, p.28.
6. M.G. Jones, *The Charity School Movement*, pp.4-5.
7. Clarke, *op. cit.*, p.41.
8. Richard D. Altick, *The English Common Reader*, p.75.
9. Mary Sturt, *The Education of the People*, p.8.
10. H.C. Barnard, *A History of English Education*, p.10.
11. Tom Paine, *Rights of Man*, 1792, Pt.2, Ch.5.
12. Altick, *op.cit.*, p.75.
13. S.H. Steinberg, *Five Hundred Years of Printing*, p.161.
14. Percy Muir, *English Children's Books, 1600-1900*, p.67.

PART 2
EDUCATIONAL PROVISION & METHODS
OF TEACHING, 1800—1850

It is difficult to form any estimation of the state of education in England at the beginning of the nineteenth century, apart from the conclusion that it was deplorably deficient. Although more schools were being provided, the number was not keeping pace with the increase in population in industrialised urban areas. Furthermore, many of the schools provided little education; the children who attended many Dame Schools would have learned more by wandering the streets. In the worst schools the doors were locked, or the children were pinned with bands of yarn to prevent them from making a dash for freedom. George Crabbe described such a school in *The Borough*, Letter 24 (1810):

> To every class we have a school assign'd,
> Rules for all ranks and food for every mind;
> Yet one there is, that small regard to rule
> Or study pays, and still is deemed a school:
> That, where a deaf, poor, patient widow sits,
> And awes some thirty infants as she knits;
> Infants of humble, busy wives, who pay
> Some trifling price for freedom through the day.

In 1838 a report to the Statistical Society of London, commenting on a survey of forty-six Dame Schools in a part of Westminster, observed that

The children are sent to these schools mainly with the view of being kept 'out of the streets', and in general read from any book which they happen to bring with them from home. A very large proportion are sent *avowedly* 'to do nothing', the injunction from the parent being that they are not to be 'worried with learning', and in some cases not even 'with needlework'.[1]

The report of the committee of the Manchester Statistical Society in 1834 had reached a similar conclusion and had stressed the appalling conditions in which the children were kept. The existence of 'one or two of the old primitive Dame Schools' was noted, however, in the 'more respectable districts'; these were more expensive; up to 7d a week. For those who could afford it, there were Day Schools; it is one of these that Crabbe describes next in *The Borough*:

To learning's second seats we now proceed,
Where humming students gilded primers read;
Or books with letters large and pictures gay,
To make their reading but a kind of play —
"Reading made Easy", so the titles tell;
But they who read must first begin to spell.

Unfortunately, many of the Common Day Schools were as bad as the Dame Schools; the teachers were generally unqualified and were often injured workmen, incompetent craftsmen, unsuccessful tradesmen or drunks. Teachers were difficult to obtain even for the more expensive Middling or Superior Day Schools.

In 1803 the Sunday School Union was founded; by then there were 7125 Sunday Schools, with 844,728 pupils. At this time it was not unusual for adults to attend to be taught to read, and many of the children attended Dame or Day Schools as well. Later in the century the education provided became more religious in character. Comments on Sunday Schools were not always favourable; James Heywood, reporting on 'the State of 176 Families in Miles Platting, within the Borough of Manchester' in 1837 observed that

It appears that the majority of the children receiving education are instructed in Sunday Schools; and it is worthy of notice that many of the children attend the Sunday-School at a very early age in Miles Platting, owing to the unwillingness of their parents to allow the elder children to attend the Sunday-School unless they take the younger children with them. Of course the maintenance of silence and order in the Sunday-Schools is rendered more difficult by the presence of a large number of infant scholars in the same room with the elder children, and the attention of the more advanced scholars must be diverted by the process of elementary instruction which is required for the infant children.[2]

There was a marked increase in the number of 'Superior' Private Schools at the beginning of the century; most girls from the Middle and Upper classes attended such schools, or were taught by governesses. The spelling book most commonly used for the education of 'superior' children at this time was Vyse's *New London Spelling Book*;

the young gentleman and lady's guide to the English tongue; containing such a variety of really useful matter, as to enable teachers to instruct their scholars to spell and read the English language with propriety, without the assistance of any other book. In which great care hs been taken to collect what may teach youth their duty and behaviour towards God and man, and avoid the numerous temptations of life, and of their own ungovernable passions.

Each letter of the alphabet is accompanied by a picture representing a nationality: O, Otaheitean; X, Xolo Islander, etc. The alphabet is then presented in a manner almost identical to that in Dyche's *Guide to the English Tongue*: columns of black letter, roman, italic, and names — a, bee, see, dee, etc. The syllabarium is larger than that in Fenning's *Universal Spelling-Book*, but the following lessons are similar: easy lessons, consisting of words not exceeding four letters:

I will mind thee, O Lord, for thou art kind to me;

followed by lists of words of one syllable, lists of words of two syllables, accented on the first, etc. The tone of the book is much more religious and moral than other spellers; the reading lessons are: Advice of a father to his children; Rules and maxims of moral conduct; On the duty of children to parents; Directions for an agreeable behaviour, polite address &c. &c. The other 'useful matter' — Introduction to the Arts and Sciences, Outlines of Geography, Survey of the Universe — is much condensed.

For younger children, the Battledore remained popular; Davison of Alnwick, Rusher of Banbury, Darton and Harvey, Dean, Mozley, and Richardson printed them into the 1830's, and there seems to have been an attempt to revive them ca. 1850, but by then new printing techniques had produced new types of alphabet books and the attempt seems to have failed.

In 1801 Sir Richard Phillips published *The English Spelling-Book*, by William Fordyce Mavor, which became the most successful of all the spelling books; the preface to the 1823 edition mentions two million copies sold in twenty-one years; the 443rd. edition (Longman) appeared in 1838; Davison and Mozley also produced editions; Routledge issued an edition illustrated by Kate Greenaway in 1885 (Spielmann and Layard considered it 'one of the most inspiring school-books ever published.'); P. Austin Nuttall edited an edition for Warne ca. 1902. The success of this book encouraged the use of the spelling method for the rest of the century although it represents a move towards phonic methods. The spelling method was to be used at least as far as lesson 14, by which time the child would have spelled out most of the three-letter words in the English language. Simple reading lessons follow, then easy words not exceeding six letters, which include rhyme, schism, czar, and drachm.

The list of words to be known at sight is longer than usual — sixty-three. A primitive phonic approach is adopted in later lessons — in a lesson on 'the E final':

All - Ale	fan - fane	mop - mope	sam - same	bab - babe
fat - fate	mor - more	sid - side		

and in 'Words of one syllable, containing the dipthongs', in which the words are listed under the appropriate dipthong —

oi - voice, choice, void, point, etc.

That the sounds of letters are considered of some importance is indicated by the section on 'Words of arbitrary sound', which includes Ache, laugh, aisle, pique and nymph. A syllabic approach is used for longer words, with the usual list of words not exceeding two syllables, and lessons in words not exceeding two syllables:

Tho-mas, what a cle-ver thing it is to read! A lit-tle while a-go, you could read on-ly lit-tle words; and you were forced to spell them, c-a-t, cat; d-o-g, dog. Now you can read pret-ty sto-ries, and I am going to tell you some.

Between the lists of three and four syllable words are fables, and lessons in natural history. The contents of the remainder of the book probably account for its popularity — there is more 'useful information' and less religious teaching than in many other spellers.

Mavor's spelling book has sometimes been called a 'Reader'. During this period, however, a Reader was a book of poems, stories or essays to be read aloud — the way the book was held, the way the child stood and the tone and clarity of the voice were all important. The child did not tackle a Reader until he had worked his way through a spelling book. A Primer at this time was a 'First Reader' — short passages with a simple vocabulary. Mavor's book had elements of the Reader and the Primer, as it had of Geography and History, but it was essentially a spelling book.

The English Spelling Book was found to be suitable for those who wished to teach themselves, but soon after its appearance other books satisfied this need, including Greig's *Expeditious Self-Instructor*;

containing the elements of Reading, Grammar, Writing, (illustrated with copies,) Arithmetic, (with tables,) Geography and the globes, History and Chronology, (with a Table,) with a great variety of Forms useful in business. The whole explained in a most familiar manner, in order to enable those to instruct themselves, who have not the opportunity of masters.

The search for political and educational enlightenment and for social betterment led to the establishment of adult education classes at Bala in 1811; by 1850, 3,500 adults were being taught to read. Reading was also taught in the Mechanics Institutes which the Utilitarian movement had promoted in 1823.

While adults were being encouraged to educate themselves, some progress was made in the provision of education of the poor, illiterate children who could not make themselves heard in Parliament. There was great interest in the work of Pestalozzi and Fellenburg, and concern over the education of the poor, but the failure of Whitbread's Bill in 1807 showed that state intervention was unacceptable. The provision of education was left to the voluntary societies.

The smaller of the two main societies was the British and Foreign School Society, originally named the Royal Lancasterian Association. Joseph Lancaster, encouraged by reading Bell's *Experiment in Education*, had used the older children in his school to teach the younger. His Quaker friends helped him publicise his methods, and men such as Wilberforce, Fry, Whitbread and Brougham were members of the Association. The National Society for promoting the Education of the Poor in the Doctrine and Discipline of the Established Church was established in 1811 as an answer to the Association; it recruited the aged Dr. Bell, who had originally advocated the monitorial system.

At first sight there does not seem to be a great difference between schools of the two societies, except perhaps that Bell used sand trays for writing on, and Lancaster used slates from old buildings. In fact, the Lancasterian Schools allowed any child to attend, no matter to what Denomination he belonged, and provided a greater range of books, and even libraries. The National Schools were for many years restricted to the Bible, Prayer Book and Catechism, or readers and spellers containing extracts from the Bible. The method of teaching reading in a monitorial school is described in Chapter 2 of Mary Sturt's book *The Education of the People*.[3] It was the spelling method in its most primitive form. Mrs. Trimmer's *Charity School Spelling Book* was used in the National Society schools — the child spelled out all the monosyllabic words in English. Having accomplished this, he progressed naturally to the syllabic method for longer words and worked his way through long lists of these until he had mastered every word in the English language that he was likely to meet. When reading began, it was conducted in exactly the same manner. The harder words were spelled out by the children in turn, the monitor spelling them out also after each child. Then each child read a word in turn until the whole passage had been read, the monitor repeating each word as it was read. Next, each child read a clause, the monitor repeating it again, and finally each sentence, great attention being paid to the stops. Little attention was paid to meaning, and since the only reading book in most schools was the Bible, the language would have been incomprehensible to most children. Later, the catechetical method was adopted in an effort to ensure that the children were aware of the meaning; the monitor would ask the question, and the other children chanting the prepared answer which had been learned by heart:

Q. What saith Solomon of oppressing the poor?
A. He that oppresseth the poor reproacheth his Maker: but he that honoureth him hath mercy on the poor. Rob not the poor, because he is poor, neither oppress the afflicted in the gate, . . . For the Lord will plead their cause, and spoil the soul of those that spoiled them.

The children would answer individually, then as a group, the whole process being repeated several times. This method was used from the start to teach the Church catechism. Sometimes the children stood in lines facing each other and took turns in questioning their partners opposite under the eye of the monitor. The more proficient children would be sent up to the master to be tested for promotion:

Thus a babel of tongues is kept going on all subjects, from Leviticus to the alphabet, in which any attempt to correct, or even to distinguish individual performances would be perfectly hopeless. One by one the more forward children are brought up to the master to 'say their lesson', which generally consists of a long column in Vyse's Spelling Book, to be said and spelt by heart, which is performed frequently with a wonderful accuracy and rapidity, and in a screech which seems expressly devised to annihilate all chance of expression or modulation of tone in reading. [4]

These methods of teaching were criticised, of course, from the start. Extreme adherence to the spelling method had been criticised by Fenning in 1767 (see Part 1). However, at the time there must have appeared little else that could be done; the National Society was taking over the Charity Schools, with their poorly-qualified staff, and the only way to cope with the large numbers of children who needed educating was by using the more advanced children to teach the rest. The spelling method was suited to these conditions; it was an accepted method, well-known to all; even the most poorly-qualified teachers could use it. It was a mechanical method; no skill or judgement was required on the part of the monitors other than the ability to decide that a child was ready to repeat a string of words at high speed. They were not called upon to decide whether a child could profitably omit certain sections of the syllabarium, or whether a child's answers were sufficiently correct for him to be promoted; the appropriate answers were set out, and would be repeated exactly. Any attempt to teach the 'powers' of the letters would have made the monitor's task extremely difficult. Moreover, there was no generally accepted phonic method in use. Attempts in this direction had to wait until training colleges for teachers had been established. Analytic methods were not considered; any attempts to arouse the interest of the children would have seemed dangerous; children's interests vary and the end-products of this system of education had to be identical, as did the end-products of the factories in which most of them were intended to work. A word method would not have been suitable for other reasons: the average length of attendance was only a year, although it rose to two years by 1850. In a year a child might master the alphabet, a large part of the syllabarium, and even a number of words to be 'known at sight'. If it met new words after leaving school, it could break the longer words into syllables, remember the syllables in the syllabarium, and make an attempt to say the word, although he would perhaps have no idea of the meaning. If it had been taught by a word method, it might have had a greater interest in reading and a limited vocabulary of simple words that it could recognise. Faced with an unknown word, it would have had no method of attack and nobody at home to help. Word methods require the presence of literate adults over a prolonged period if they are to be really effective, and this neither the schools nor the child's home environment could offer.

Both the National Society and the British and Foreign School Society were aware of the need for a well-trained body of teachers in schools for the poor, yet neither society could afford efficient Training Colleges. Lancaster's school at Borough Road had a Normal School attached to it, and the National Society established one at Westminster, but the training they offered was merely of two or three weeks on the organisation of the monitorial system. Better training than this had to wait until the Committee of Council was established in 1839.

In the preceding years arguments over state control of education continued. Brougham's Committee in 1818 emphasised the lack of provision; only 1 in 16 of the total population attended school, not counting the Dame Schools; a proportion of 1 in 8 was considered desirable. 3,500 parishes were without any kind of school. These figures may be unreliable; many schools were ephemeral. Evidence of educational provision during this period is often conflicting, as Roger Sellman has recently pointed out.[5] Nevertheless, the lack of schools was constantly brought to the notice of the public. Brougham's Parish School Bill of 1820 failed, but agitation continued. His pamphlet *Observations on the Education of the People* led to the founding of the Society for the Diffusion of Useful Knowledge in 1825. The passing of the Reform Bill in 1832 gave power to the middle classes, and the need for popular education appeared greater than ever. Roebuck's measure of 1833 was withdrawn, but the Government voted £20,000 for the erection of school houses. The voluntary societies were to spend the money; the Government was not willing to take control of education. By the mid 1830's there were approximately 1,000,000 children in attendance at National Society Schools and 70,000 at British and Foreign School Society Schools. Sunday School attendance was somewhere between 800,000 and 1,500,000.

A clear idea of the quality of the education provided is difficult to obtain. The state of education in Westminster was the subject of reports to a committee of the London Statistical Society in 1838,[6] and these give interesting accounts of the types of school, attendance and books used. In the first two parishes, St. John and St. Margaret, probably 3,000 children had no instruction whatsoever. 3,655 attended Day or Evening Schools only; 1542 Sunday as well as Day Schools; and 586 Sunday Schools only; a total of 5,783. The weather affected the attendance at Dame and Common Day Schools. 721 children attended the 63 Dame Schools, paying between 2d. and 8d. a week. 296 of these children were under five years old, none were over fifteen. Spelling and reading were professed to be taught, but 'nearly half have not advanced beyond the first study'. Books, other than a Bible or Testament, spelling-books or primers, were rarely found. In some instances there was only one book in the school; in others, any book brought by the children was made use of. Thirty of the teachers took in needlework, or kept a shop or dairy. Only twelve had been 'brought up to the profession of teaching'.

The 41 Common Day Schools charged between 4d. and a shilling a week. 954 children attended — 185 under five, and only three over fifteen. 812 were learning to read, the remainder to spell. In several schools the only book met with was the Bible or Testament, others had primers and spelling-books as well; some had Watt's Hymns, Pinnock's Catechisms etc. The Middling Day Schools charged between 10/- and 31/6 a quarter; French, Latin and Music were extra.

There were 20 such schools; 602 children attended, 20 of them under five and 23 over fifteen. 633 children attended 6 Infant Schools; 218 of them were over five years old. There were only 4 Superior Day Schools, with 88 children, all aged between five and fifteen. The Charity Schools numbered only 23, but 2,085 children were in attendance; 60 under five, and 16 over 15. 360 children were learning to spell, 1689 were learning to read, and 1572 were learning to write. Books found in these schools were the Old and New Testament, Watts' catechism, cards of the British and Foreign System, Primers, Markham's, Windett's, the Universal and Sunday School Spelling Books. The Superior Day Schools used the Bible and Testament, Barbauld's Prose Hymns, Watts' Divine Songs, Mavor's, Carpenter's and Guy's Spelling Books, Guy's Questions and Lennie's Child's Ladder. The books found in the Middling Day Schools were the Bible and Testament, Barrow's Questions, Watt's Divine Songs, Barbauld's Hymns in Prose, Mavor's, Carpenter's, Robinson's, Vyse's, Guy's, the Universal and Bible Spelling Books, Primers, Carpenter's and Cobbins's English Vocabularies, and Cobbin's Instructive Readers. The list of books found in the Dame and Common Day Schools is given in a table; the numbers refer to the number of copies found, not the number of schools using the books.

In Dame Schools, single copies were found of Original Poems for Infants, Mama's Gift of Amusement, Scripture Lessons, a Moral Song Book, and Explanation of Collects.

	Dame	Common Day
Bible and Testament:	21	31
Testament:	20	5
Prayer Book:	2	
Catechisms:	5	5
Watts' Hymns:	10	5
Primers, Various:	24	15
Spelling Books:		
Universal	13	5
Guy's	8	15
Mavor's	16	27
Vyse's	23	16
Carpenter's	3	19
Fenning's	2	2
New London	5	1
Cobbett's	1	
Innes's Minerva	1	1
Alphabets, Various:	11	1
Good Child's Book:	2	
Windett's Reading and Spelling:	1	
First Class Book:	1	
Little Red Riding Hood:	1	
Hewlett's Reading Made Easy	1	1
Sunday School Books, Various:	11	1

No details are given of the books used in Evening Schools; there were 15 of these schools, usually kept by masters of the Common Day Schools. 686 children attended, most of whom were under fifteen, and they paid between 6d. and a shilling a week. The books found in the Infant Schools were Primers, cards of the Infant School Union, Bilby's and Ridways's books and cards, and spelling-books. 2128 children attended 13 Sunday Schools, of whom 1542 attended Day Schools also. 437 children were under five, and 23 over fifteen. Instruction in these schools was confined to reading the Scriptures, with the exception of four schools which taught spelling to a few children.

The third report,[7] on other parishes, gives a similar picture, and adds that

The Bible and Testament seem to be universally used in both the Common and Middling Day Schools as *class books,* or books in which the children learn to spell and read.

Among the books listed in this report that were not in the last are Entick's Dictionary, United Brethren's Text-Book, Dr. Mablin's Reading Easy, Davies' Reading Made Easy, Murray's Introduction to Reading, and Murray's Grammar. In addition, 27 copies of abridgements of Murray's Grammar were found in Common Day Schools. The cheaper grammars were used by some children: the section on Orthography dealt with the letters of the alphabet, the formation of syllables, and the spelling of words.

Later reports of the Statistical Society of London on the state of education in Pendleton, West Bromwich and Rutland[8] stress that although the children appeared to make considerable progress in reading while they attended school, few had any understanding of what they read.

The effects of the educational provisions of the Factories' Act was also the subject of a report, and the following extract will show how ineffecive they were:

One great obstacle to the improvement of the system of education, not only in factories but in the country generally, is the want of good schoolmasters. To this point both Mr. Horner and Mr. Saunders call attention: the former states that "it is not at all an unusual thing to have certificates presented to us subscribed by the teacher with his or her *mark*. this generally happens in the case of female teachers; but they are held to be equal in qualification to the majority of those who keep 'dame schools' In the last quarter I had a school-voucher presented to me with a *mark*, and when I called on the schoolmaster to read it before me, he could not. It had been written out by the clerk of the factory, and the schoolmaster had been called to put his mark on it I have had to reject the school-voucher of the fireman. the children having been schooled in the coal-hole (in one case I actually found them there), and having been made to say a lesson, from books nearly as black as the fuel, in the interval between his feeding and stirring the fire of the engine-boiler It may be supposed that such a thing could only happen at the mill of some poor ignorant man; but that, I am sorry to say, was not the case, for it occurred at factories where a large capital must be embarked."

Mr Barker quotes several instances of the incapacity of the teachers, of which the two following certificates afford a specimen:

1   "This to sertfy that 1838 thomas Cordingley as atend martha insep school tow hours per day January 6."

2   "Sir The reason P Harrison left me I suppose to be his objection to pay my demands, as he left me in arrears Elizth Northern has not and will not pay me a penny ever since she came to me; her plea is that you stop it out of her wage. – If you please Sir. If you plase Fairplay's a Jewel. *E Hinchcliffe* "

Mr Barker adds "Factory-schools are of many kinds, from the coal-hole of the engine-house to the highest grade of infant education. The engine-man, the slubber, the burler, the book-keeper, the overlooker, the wife of any of these, the small shopkeeper, or the next-door neighbour, with six or seven small children on the floor and in her lap, are by turns found teaching the young idea how to shoot,' in and about their several places of occupation for the two hours required by the law. Few, how few, good schools are here and there bestowing upon so important a community as the manufacturing classes the benefits of the national system of education and of moral training, to fit them for their future station, and impress them with its relative duties! I do not think that, among the 500 mills under my superintendence in the West Riding of Yorkshire, I should be able to name a dozen schools where the education is systematically good, and the mill-owner personally cognizant of the progress of his children   9

Although the picture presented by these reports is somewhat gloomy, progress was being made. There was a great interest in the teaching of reading, which is shown by the variety of alphabet books, primers, and spelling books which appear. No real progress was made, however, until the Committee of Council was established in 1839. Kay-Shuttleworth was appointed as Secretary, and he established a Training College at Battersea. By 1845 there were twenty-two Church Training Colleges in England and Wales. The Government grant for education had been renewed annually, and had increased. The Committee of Council appointed Inspectors who, although they had no power to interfere with the running of a school, could report back to the Council and offer advice. The inspectors were loud in their condemnation of the monitorial system, and the simultaneous system which had come into use in Scotland was gradually adopted in English schools. The master took 'intellectual teaching' — questioning, moral, or general knowledge questions; at the same time he could watch over writing or arithmetic being done by another class; the third class did reading and spelling, supervised by monitors — about ten children to a monitor. In 1846 the Committee of Council recommended the establishment of the pupil-teacher system. The first examinations were held in 1847, and by 1849 there were 681 certificated teachers in schools. The Committee were aware of the need of

The compilation and publication of a complete set of good school books which from their cheapness, independently altogether of their excellence, which the great majority of the people are still incapable of appreciating, would find their way into the hands of every schoolboy. It would be difficult to mention anything the accomplishment of which would have a more extensive and beneficial influence upon elementary education.10

Such books were not forthcoming, although the Commissioners of National Education for Ireland had commissioned text-books which became increasingly popular in this country. The Committee at first refused to give grants for books, but in 1847 issued schedules of books which were considered suitable for use by schools, and which could be obtained at a discount. The list of Reading Lesson Books is given below; the schedules also gave size, binding, cost, etc.

Educational Books —
   The First Book
   The Second Book
   The Third Book

Society for Promoting Christian Knowledge.

Reading Series —
  No. 1
  No. 2

Society for Promoting Christian Knowledge.

These books are in use chiefly in Church of England Schools connected with the National Society.

Moral and Intellectual Series —
  No. 1, Daily Lesson Book.
  No. 2, ditto
  No. 3, ditto
  No. 4, ditto
  Sequel to No. 1, or
    No. 1, in sheets.
  Sequel to ditto, No. 2

Compiled by some of the chief officers of the British and Foreign School Society.

These books are in general use in schools for the British and Foreign School Society.

The Reading Lesson Books —
  The First.
  The Second.
  The Third.
  The Fourth.
  The Fifth.
Sequel to Second.
  Supplement to Fourth.
  Reading Book for the use of female Schools.

Compiled and published under the authority of the Commissioners of National Education in Ireland.

These Reading Lesson Books were compiled for the National School established under the Board of Education in Ireland, but they are also extensively in use among all classes of schools in England, Wales and Scotland.

First Reading Book
  Second ditto
  Third ditto
  Series of Lessons in Prose and Verse.
  Course of Elementary Reading.

By the Rev. J. M. M'Culloch, LL.D.

Dr. M'Culloch's Series of Reading Lessons is in very general use in efficient middle-class schools, and the best Parochial and other elementary Schools, in the north of England and Scotland. As their character has become known in midland and southern counties of England, they have had a constantly increasing sale.

Rural Spelling Book.

By C.W. Johnson, F.R.S.

The New Series of School Books—
  The Child's First Book.
  No. 1, Primer.
  No. 2, Second Lessons.
  No. 3, Third ditto
  Manual of English Pronunciation, or Sequel to Third Lessons.
  Sheet Lessons.
  No. 4, Readings in Prose and Verse.
  No. 5, First collection of Instructive Extracts.
  No. 6, Second collection of Instructive Extracts.
  Reprints of Vocabularies from Nos. 5 & 6.

Compiled for the Scottish School-Book Association.

This new series has been compiled under the super-intendence of the Scottish Schoolmaster's Association and may be regarded as the work of the most intelligent members of that body. The use of these books is becoming more general in the parochial and private schools of Scotland.

No. 1, Lessons for Schools.
No. 2, ditto
No. 3, ditto
No. 4, ditto

By the late Rev. A. Thomson, D.D.

Compiled by the late Rev. Dr. Andrew Thomson, of Edinburgh, an eminent divine of the Scottish Church. The circulation of these books is nearly confined to the Sessional Schools of Scotland.

The Juvenile Reader.

By Neil Leitch.

A Reading Book for the first or second class of an elementary school used in Scotland.

Reading Disentangled;
  being a series of Elementary Reading Lessons on Sheets.

By the author of "Peep of Day."

In very general use for the instruction of very young children in reading in all classes of Elementary Schools.

The acceptance of these books into English schools is evidence of the gradual abandonment of the Spelling method. The syllabarium continued to be taught in many schools, and protests were still heard — how could see, ay, tee, spell cat? Difficult or unknown words still had to be spelled out before reading began. The standard procedure for many was that advocated in the preface to an American book, *The Juvenile Reader*:[11]

The practice of teaching a child to read before he is familiar with the orthography and pronunciation of words, is productive of great injury, and tends to retard rather than facilitate correct reading. No person should attempt to read until he is able to call or pronounce at sight the words most commonly met with in composition; and, this can be more easily acquired by reading words in a judicious and analogical classification in a Spelling Book, than in detached reading lessons.

After the syllabarium had been learned, the child no longer spelled the familiar words aloud; he named the letters silently, and came to recognise the words without breaking them down into their elements:

The author would respectfully suggest the propriety of accustoming the child to pronounce the words in the spelling lessons, without naming the letters, until he shall be quite familiar with them.

The spelling method was bitterly attacked by the inspectors; it appeared inextricably linked with the monitorial system. The contents of reading books had to be made more interesting, and a more efficient and less frustrating method of teaching reading was needed. Henry Dunn, secretary of the British and Foreign School Society, said in his *Principles of Teaching* (1837) that 'The principle of dispensing with alphabetic teaching has long been adopted' — a very misleading statement. He probably meant that there was no longer an insistence in schools on the spelling out by name of all the letters of every word that the child read in school — much more attention was being given to the sounds of the letters; indeed the spelling method was to merge eventually with phonic methods. More encouragement was given to the child to recognise words at sight. Methods of teaching reading were becoming diverse, and Dunn was probably stressing the fact that a rigid spelling method was no longer in use. The books listed in the 1847 schedules represented no new departure in teaching methods; the spelling method was being modified, but analytic methods were still ignored. The *Second Book of Lessons*, compiled for the Commissioners of National Education in Ireland begins:

boy	stand	hair
girl	wrong	noise
comb	school	learnt
hand	home	good
know	wash	class

Boys and girls must not play all day. So comb your hair, and wash your hands, and come to school. Stand up in your class; you can read some words now . . . .

The words above the lessons had to be learned before reading began; how they were learned depended upon the inclination of the teacher. They could be spelled out, reference could be made to the sounds of the letters, or they could be remembered from their shapes. No doubt many children used the last method, but as Huey pointed out:[10]

The manner in which a word is perceived will depend, for a child, very largely on how he is *taught* to perceive them in learning to read.

The children of the 1840's were usually taught to perceive words by identifying the letters. This method has sometimes been called a word method, but must not be confused with analytic methods; it is distinctly alphabetic: a development of the spelling method, with some reference to phonics. The thinking behind this method is summed up in a later book, *Hand-Book of School Management and Methods of Teaching:*

In learning the alphabet, three things have to be mastered; first, the shapes of the letters; second, their names; third, their powers or sounds. The names of the letters are perfectly distinct from their sounds in words . . . . . The child has to learn not only the names of the letters, but also the additional and totally different fact, that when they are put together, they make the sound *top* . . . . Formerly a child was obliged to learn the whole alphabet before he was put to spell the simplest words. We follow a different plan: we break up the alphabet into parcels, and as soon as the child has learned a certain number of letters, he is taught to apply them at once to the spelling of little words.[13]

The only difference between this method of the 1860's and the method under review is that the alphabet was broken down 'into parcels'. Reading did not begin until the words were known; it was not an analytic method. It was not a true phonic method; the names of the letters were learned first, no account was taken of digraphs and the letters were not put into 'parcels' on a phonic basis.

Efforts to make the teaching of reading more efficient led to the Spelling Dictionaries which presented long lists of words to be learned and spelled to the master. The more words that a child could spell, the more he would recognise in his reading lessons. Sometimes diacritical marks were added to the words as an aid to pronunciation, as in Carpenter's *Spelling Assistant*, which was originally published in 1796, but became popular after 1830. Other books arranged the words according to the sound of the vowel in the accented syllable. The most successful book of this type was Butter's *Etymological Spelling Book and Expositor*, first published in 1830, which reached its 421st edition in 1883, and was reprinted in 1941. Books which contained dictation exercises to test the child's knowledge of the words were a natural consequence — books such as Bearcroft's *Practical Orthography*;

or, the art of teaching spelling by writing; containing an improved method of dictating, with exercises for practice; and collections of words of difficult, irregular, and variable spelling.

While the spelling method was gradually becoming indistinguishable from phonic methods, the latter were developing separately. In 1801 a teacher named Kay published *The New Preceptor*, which described a phonic method which he had been using in his own school. The children named the letters according to their sounds, and then sounded out the letters of the syllabarium instead of naming them. Consonants were presented as 'mutes' — which could not make a perfect sound without a vowel, and 'semivowels' — which could make an imperfect sound alone. The double letters ch, ph, sh, th, and wh were to be named as single characters.

The next attempt to present a phonic method was more successful; Helen Maria Williams's *Summary Method of Teaching Children to Read*, which was first published in 1817, appeared in a cheap edition in 1819, and was still in print under the title of *Syllabic Spelling* in the 1830's. It attracted enough attention for other authors to write readers 'adapted to Mrs. Williams' Syllabic Method.' In fact, it was an adaption of a French method: 'discovered by the Sieur Berthaud'. Letters and syllables were presented with pictures; the child named the object in the picture, and the first sound of the word was the sound of the accompanying letter or syllable.

After the establishment of the Committee of Council, inspectors were insistent that teachers should be made aware of methods of teaching reading other than their own. The phonic methods in use in Germany and America were quoted, and lecturers at the training college at Battersea experimented with the phonic method at some London schools. In the method used at Battersea, the child first drew the letter, then named it by its sound. When the vowels had been learned they were placed before and after consonants, and these combinations were written by the child and then pronounced. Next, vowels were placed between two consonants and this combination was pronounced. Soon after this, the child began to write simple sentences; reading was not introduced until the child had mastered the sounds of letters and phonograms, by which time he should have been able to read any regular word. The phonic reading book excluded irregular words as much as possible. The immediate effect of the efforts at Battersea was a further modification of the spelling method, with greater emphasis being placed on the sounds of letters, but after 1850 more phonic readers appeared. The most influential was *Reading Without Tears*, by Favell Lee Mortimore, published by Hatchards, who were the publishers also of *Stepping-Stones for Tottering Feet*, an earlier phonic reader. The publication of *Reading Without Tears* in 1850 marked a change in the teaching of reading; it was the first successful phonic method to be widely accepted in this country, and survived into this century.

The spelling method, although it underwent changes, remained the normal method of teaching reading until 1850. There were other variations which were tried at times; Dr. Andrew Thompson in Scotland broke the alphabet into groups of letters according to their shape; Professor James Pillans of Edinburgh arranged his groups according to the sounds of the letters, and described his method in *Principles of Elementary Teaching* (1828). This was a near-phonic method, but the letters were still named. After 1850 the spelling method was still used; it persisted into this century in some schools, and of course is still with us in the alphabet books which parents buy for their children in vast quantities every year.

In spite of encouragement from the inspectors, no attempt was made to introduce analytic methods. Efforts to make education more interesting and meaningful did not include the adoption of methods of teaching reading which stress meaning from the start. Perhaps it was too great a step to take — the spelling method was gradually transformed into a phonic method over a period of years, and the change from a synthetic to an analytic method would have meant a sudden innovation. Word methods were known and discussed; Dunn mentioned Jacatot favourably in *Principles of Teaching* [14] in 1837. In America, Worcester's *Primer of the English Language* (1828) and McGuffey's *Readers* (1836) had introduced word methods. These books were referred to favourably by the inspectors, but were not copied in this country.

An English method, however, was tried out in America. A.J. Ellis and Isaac Pitman devised a 'phonetic print' which they called Phonotypy, which was designed to teach children to read. In 1845 *The Phonographic and Phonotypic Alphabets* was published. The system was tried in schools in England, but attracted no attention. Later, it was tried out in Massachusetts over a period of five years. There is obviously a close connection between Shorthand and phonic or phonetic methods of teaching during this period; Mavor's *Universal Stenography* had reached its fifth edition by 1801, and the next few years saw new books or systems by Clive, Molineux, Williams, Prosser, Hodson, Harwin, Richardson, Sams, Hunter, Duncan, Gardiner, Gawtress, Farr, Harding, Walker, Lindley Murray, Hinton, Enfield, Carstairs, Jones, Moat, Macdougal, Whitehead, Foster Floyd, to name but a few. Pitman's alphabet led, of course to ita, but other phonetic methods were discarded by teachers of reading.

The year 1850 marked the end of a period of great change in Education in England. By the time that Kay-Shuttleworth retired in 1849 the pupil-teacher system had been established, phonic methods were becoming generally accepted, and the State was taking a greater interest in Education. It seemed to many that enough had been done, and that it was time to pause and to consider what exactly were the results of the system of elementary education that had been provided.

NOTES

1. *Journal of the Statistical Society of London,* Vol.1 (1838), p. 451.
2. *Ibid.,* p.148.
3. Mary Sturt, *The Education of the People,* Routledge & Kegan Paul, 1967.
4. *Parliamentary Papers,* 1847, 27, Pt.2, p.29.
5. Roger R. Sellman, *Devon Village Schools in the 19th. Century,* p.29.
6. *Journal of the Statistical Society of London,* Vol.1 (1838), p.193ff., p.449ff.
7. *Ibid.,* p.450.
8. *Journal of the Statistical Society of London,* Vol.2, Chas. Knight & Co., 1839.
9. *Ibid.,* p.179.
10. *Minutes of the Committee of Council on Education,* 1840-1, p.177.
11. Lyman Cobb, *Juvenile Reader No. 1,* New York, 1831.
12. E.B. Huey, *The Psychology and Pedagogy of Reading,* MacMillan, New York, 1908, Pt.1, p.103.
13. P.W. Joyce, *A Handbook of School Management and Methods of Teaching,* Simpkin, Marshal & Co., 2nd Ed., 1864, p.119.
14. Henry Dunn, *Principles of Teaching,* Sunday School Union, etc., c.1850.

PART 3
THE EFFECTIVENESS OF THE METHODS

The methods of education adopted by the voluntary societies did not produce the results that had been envisaged at the beginning of the century. There was still a great lack of skilled workers and the unskilled did not accept their lowly position with suitable meekness. The new lower-class reading public that was being created resented the tracts that were designed to keep them content with their dreadful conditions.[1] As early as 1833 the S.P.C.K. was worried that the population was

for the first time becoming a reading population, actuated by tastes and habits unknown to preceding generations and particularly susceptible to such an influence as that of the press.[2]

The size of the reading public at any period before 1850 is difficult to determine. An estimation might be made by consulting the few statistics, or by considering the growth of the publishing and printing industries and examining their products. A statistical examination can be extremely misleading, since the figures are often unreliable, particularly in the cases of Dame Schools and factories. The Factory Act of 1833 led to the establishment of schoolrooms where children were educated for two hours a day. Factory owners claimed that the majority of children were being taught to read. However, as we have seen, the rooms were often coal-holes and the teachers usually unqualified. The Children's Employment Commission in 1842 noted that any child who knew his alphabet was stated to be learning to read.

The varying definitions of literacy make estimation difficult. In some cases children were classed as illiterate if they were unable to write, yet many of the children who left school could read simple English although they could not write it. Sometimes ability to read the Bible was the criterion, yet many children left school before they reached that standard; a comparison of reports from schools of the 1840's indicates that approximately 18% of children in attendance could read the Bible, whereas 33% could read simple narratives.

Statistics on the provision of schools can also be misleading, as has already been indicated in Part 1. Many of the schools at the beginning of the century were ephemeral in nature, and although the numbers of children in attendance increased after the establishment of the voluntary societies, it must be remembered that the population of the country doubled during the first half of the century. Brougham's Committee of 1818 had indicated that a figure of 1 in 8 of the population was a desirable figure for school attendance. In 1800 the ratio had been 1 in 21, in 1858 it was 1 in 7.83. This figure takes no account of the quality of education, nor of the fact that the length of attendance might only be a few months.[3]

Although the number of children in attendance at any time was low, children remained at school for only a short period, and the number of children who passed through the schools might have been quite high. In the Miles Platting survey, only 288 out of 505 children attended school, and, of these, 208 attended only Sunday Schools. Of the 217 who did not attend school, some may have attended in later years. If the average length of attendance was only eighteen months, some may have been in attendance in earlier years and have been withdrawn. Although the survey was critical of the state of literacy of the adult population, 130 of the 176 heads of families 'professed to be able to read', and 5 more 'read imperfectly.'[4]

Other statistics from this period indicate, as might be expected, that the standard of literacy was higher among children than among adults. In 1837 Sir James Kay-Shuttleworth, who was then James Phillip Kay, Assistant Poor-Law Commissioner, examined 'Some of the results of the previously existing system of instruction upon the intelligence of the pauperised classes.'[5] In the Norfolk and Suffolk Unions, 39% of those above the age of sixteen could read, either 'In a superior manner', 'Decently', or 'Imperfectly'. In the twelve East Kent Unions, 51% could read. The table showing 'The state of instruction of the children in the workhouses, even after some improvements have been effected in the schools' indicates that 67% of the children aged between two and sixteen could read 'well' or 'imperfectly'. However, exact figures concerning the level of literacy are difficult to obtain; to form a better idea of the growth of the reading public, developments in the publishing and printing industries must be studied.

Before 1800, little change had been made in the design of the printing press since Gutenberg had adapted the Roman wine press. The wooden screw had been replaced by one of iron, and the type area had been doubled, but the press remained essentially unchanged. After 1800 there were rapid developments — beginning with Stanhope's iron press of 1804. The Albion, with a knuckle joint and spring, appeared in 1817, and could produce 270 sheets an hour. In 1818 the Times was printed on a power press at the rate of 1,100 sheets an hour. The cylinder press was patented in the same year. In 1829, stereotyping was perfected; this led to the development of the rotary press. After 1840, photography expanded the use of the lithographic press, which had first appeared in London in 1810.

There were also developments in allied industries which helped to produce larger editions at lower prices. In 1803, the Fourdrinier brothers perfected a machine which made paper ten times faster than the old mills. By 1824 the cost of paper had fallen by a third; in 1843, by a half. Cloth began to replace leather for binding in 1820, and in 1830 machine binding was introduced. A letter-founding machine was developed in 1822 which could produce up to 20,000 letters a day instead of the 7,000 maximum by hand. Developments were made in the printing of illustrations; half-tone blocks were in use from 1837, and after 1835 printed colour pictures began to replace hand-coloured plates in more expensive books.

Not all the inventions can be said to derive from the technical progress which followed the Industrial Revolution. Many had been suggested at an earlier date. In Da Vinci's notebooks, not published until 1797, can be found details of a press which closely resembles Stanhope's iron press. Suggestions for making paper from wood pulp were put forward in 1719 and 1732. Stereotyping had been developed in the late seventeenth century. Sometimes inventions had not been adopted through inertia, sometimes through hostility. Before 1800, innovations had been resented.[6] After 1800 they were willingly accepted in most cases; there was a demand for books which could not be met by traditional methods.

An excellent example of the interaction of printing and local culture can be seen in the history of the Soulby family of Ulverston. Before the appearance of the first press in the town, notices had to be put up on the market cross.[7] By 1817, John Soulby, senior, had established a library and a shop selling patent medicines, perfumes, stationery and drawing materials, and had built up a printing business which produced notices, handbills, billheads, posters, trade cards, receipts, playbills; in fact, all the productions of a jobbing printer which a literate community demands. After Soulby's death in 1817, his trustees continued the business. His eldest son, John, established his own press, and other printers were at work in Ulverston. Stephen Soulby, a younger son, printed the Ulverston Almanack. After the reduction of the stamp duty on newspapers in 1836, many small printers began to produce local newspapers. Stephen published the Ulverston Advertiser in 1842, but found that the effort of producing a weekly paper put too great a strain on his business; he designed a cylinder press which was built in 1852.[8] This press was soon superseded, but is an example of the technical progress which was trying to keep pace with the demands of a new literate public.

An examination of the output of the Soulby presses makes clear that they were fulfilling a need, not creating a demand. The articles that were sold in the Soulby shop indicate a spreading of literacy in the middle classes. Many other towns had printers and booksellers who established circulating libraries, following the advice of James Lackington. Experience proved that the sale of books was promoted by these libraries; they encouraged the production of Gothick novels, love stories, and the works of Walter Scott and other 'three-decker' novelists. Large publishing houses supplied the demand; smaller printers remained jobbing printers, and since their work was ephemeral in nature, much of it has disappeared, surviving only in collections such as that of the late Dr. John Johnson, which has now been acquired by the Bodleian Library. Despite the poor quality of education, literacy during this period was becoming widespread; small printers encouraged the teaching of reading by printing an extraordinary number of alphabet and spelling books, but there was obviously a steady profit to be made from such material.

The growth of the reading habit among the middle classes is well documented. Children of these classes were becoming sufficiently literate to read for pleasure. William Roscoe's *Butterfly's Ball* (1807) and Catherine Sinclair's *Holiday*

House (1839) were notable examples of this trend, but by the 1850's, children were reading Marryat's.*Children of the New Forest* and *Masterman Ready.* The educational methods of the 1840's produced a younger reading public with a thirst for books of adventure or fantasy, avid readers of Charles Kingsley, W.H.G. Kingston, Hans Anderson, and Edward Lear. Some efforts were made to satisfy the demands of lower class children. The Religious Tract Society had attempted to copy the format of the chapbook, but the true descendants of the chap book in this period were the cheap children's books produced by firms such as Oliver and Boyd — their 'Juvenile Books' included Sermons for Children, Moral Tales and Principles of Religion, but the majority were up-to-date versions of old chapbook favourites, including Bluebeard, The Seven Champions of Christendom, Jack the Giant-Killer, and Cock Robin's Death and Burial.

Adult reading followed a similar pattern. The sales of Scott's novels set new records; a total of 6,000 copies of *Waverley* were sold in six months in 1814; 40,000 copies of *Rob Roy* before 1836. Dickens' *Pickwick Papers* were selling at the rate of 40,000 copies per issue when Part 15 appeared.[9] The readers of this type of fiction were the skilled workers, shopkeepers, clerks and superior servants. The lowest classes had their fiction too, but less attention has been paid to this, and only in recent years have attempts been made to preserve it.

Whereas the middle classes were growing increasingly prosperous, and regarded reading as an occupation to fill their leisure hours, the lower classes read to escape from the tedium of their occupations. The penny-issue novel was their staple diet, and numerous pirated and amended editions of Dickens' work appeared. In an effort to counteract the effect of *The Penny Magazine* (1832) which had a circulation of 200,000 by the end of the year, the S.P.C.K. issued *The Saturday Magazine* for the upper classes, and claimed to have sold 45,000,000 copies in the first four months.?[10] Estimates for the numbers of periodicals costing twopence or less circulating every month gave the figures of 75,000 for Birmingham and 57,000 for Manchester.[11]   After 1840, the mass of cheap literature tor bored minds became more sensational. There was an increase in pornography, and the lower-class 'penny dreadfuls' of the 1830's were becoming children's literature.

This phenomenal increase in cheap literature, together with accounts of libraries which were established in public houses, barracks, shops, factories, Churches, Chapels, and Sunday, Ragged and Factory Schools, seems hard to reconcile with complaints of the lack of education, or its ineffectiveness. In fact, the education provided for most children consisted of a grounding in literacy. Although attendance figures were small, the fact that many children spent only a year or two at school may mean, as I have previously indicated, that many more passed through than has been estimated.

A typical comment on the results of the education of this period is that made in the Miles Platting survey:

There are very few of the heads of the families, included within this enquiry, who have formed the habit of reading, or are capable of understanding or enjoying a book. Many are either too illerate, or too deeply sunken in indifference, or in animal gratification, to be easily convinced of the importance of the mental culture of religion.[12]

Nevertheless, 130 of the 176 heads of families 'professed to be able to read.' They were not in the habit of reading — the spelling method did not encourage this habit, and the spelling method was still in use, although considerably modified, in 1850. In the 1870's, Inspectors complained that 80% of children left school before they had reached 'a standard high enough to be of permanent benefit'; before 1850, the percentage must have been much higher. 'Permanent benefit' seems to have meant that the child had reached a stage sufficiently advanced to enable him to maintain an interest in reading, coupled with the ability to make further progress on his own. There is no doubt that the education provided in schools between 1800 and 1850 did little to foster a child's interest in reading; certainly, not in the way hoped for. Nevertheless, it is obvious that children did develop the habit of reading; the middle classes read adventure stories tinged with piety, the lower classes, the 'penny dreadfuls'.

The spelling method was criticised because it was inefficient — at a time when efficiency was particularly needed because educational provision was so lacking, and this led to the gradual adoption of phonic methods. Criticisms that the spelling method left the child uninterested in reading were later transferred to phonic methods, which in turn were to give way to analytic methods which stressed meaning from the start. Despite the criticisms, it would appear that the spelling method in a pure or modified form did much to establish basic literacy in this country. It is impossible to say now how children learned to read — whether they used the spelling method, were taught a phonic approach, developed their own, or whether they recognised words as wholes, either by responding to the constituent letters or by outline — but children were presented with letters and words and learned to recognise them.

The great changes in reading habits among the lower classes in the first half of the nineteenth century — from small editions of chapbooks to enormous editions of penny fiction — and the evolution among the middle classes of a new type of reader who demanded books like *Coral Island* and *Swiss Family Robinson*, indicate that the methods of teaching reading, whatever their faults, were more effective than has been generally supposed.

NOTES

1. Richard D. Altick, *The English Common Reader*, p.93.
2. S.P.C.K. *Minutes* (1832), pp.284-5.
3. *Newcastle Report*, Vol.1, p.87.
4. *Journal of the Statistical Society of London,* Vol.1 (1838), p.148.
5. *Ibid.*, p.14.
6. S.H. Steinberg, *Five Hundred Years of Printing*, p.190.
7. Michael Twyman, *John Soulby, Printer, Ulverston*, p.17.
8. James S. Dearden, "This printer-inventor almost made history", *Small Printer*, No.18, June 1966, p.16.
9. Altick, *op.cit.*, p.383.
10. Louis James, *Fiction for the Working Man*, pp.45ff.
11. *Ibid.*, p.20.
12. *Journal of the Statistical Society of London*, Vol.1 (1838) p.149.

Facsimile Pages

THE ALPHABET

Hornbook. The traditional method of teaching reading, in use from 1450. By 1800 the hornbook usually displayed only the alphabet. See page 4.

Wood-cut Alphabet. A typical alphabet sheet of the late 18th. or early 19th. century. Some were beautifully engraved, others extremely crude.

Battledore. *A New Invented Horn Book* (c.1770-75), reproduced by permission of Messrs. Sotheby Parke Bernet & Co. Battledores, based on the hornbook, were attractive folded cards with a few simple illustrations. Introduced in 1750, they were printed by the thousand, and sold for a penny each. By 1850 they had given way to the Victorian colour-printed alphabets. See page 8.

ABCDEFGHIKLMN
OPQRSTUWXYZ.
abcdefghiklmnopqrsſtuvwxyz ꝫꞇ.
✠ a e i o u ✠ a e i o u ✠
ab eb ib ob ub ‖ ba be bi bo bu
ac ec ic oc uc ‖ ca ce ci co cu
ad ed id od ud ‖ da de di do du

In the Name of the Father/and of the
Sonne/and of the holy Ghost. Amen.

¶ Our Father which art in heaven/
hallowed bee thy Name. Thy
Kingdome come. Thy will be
done in earth as it is in heaven. ✠
Giue vs this day our daily bredd.
And forgiue vs our trespalles/as
we forgiue them that trespalleys.
And let vs not bee ledd into temp-
tation: but deliuer vs from euill:
Amen. i. ii. iii. iiii. v. vi. vii. viii. ix. x.

Wood-cut Alphabet

A new invented Horn Book

a b c d e f g h i j k l m n o
p q r ſ s t u v w x y z.

A B C D E F G H I J K L M N O
P Q R S T U V W X Y Z.

a e i o u y.

ab eb ib ob ub	ba be bi bo bu by
ac ec ic oc uc	ca ce ci co cu cy
ad ed id od ud	ga ge gi go gu gy
ag eg ig og ug	ja je ji jo ju jy

The LORD's PRAYER.

OUR Father which art in Heaven, hallowed be thy name;
thy kingdom come; thy will be
done in earth as it is in Heaven:
Give us this day our daily bread:
And forgive us our treſpaſſes, as
we forgive them that treſpaſs a-
gainſt us; and lead us not into
temptation, but deliver us from
evil. For thine is the kingdom,
the power and the glory, for ever
and ever. *Amen.*

Battledore

SPELLING-BOOKS

Vyse's *New London Spelling-Book*; an 18th. century 'old-fashioned' Speller which remained in print throughout the period. This Speller was an all-purpose text-book, and included Fables, a Guide to Grammar, Rules of Moral Conduct, Lessons in Natural History, a Brief Introduction to the Arts and Sciences, Outlines of History and Geography, and Tables. See page 18.

Mavor's *English Spelling-Book*; the main 19th. century Speller, first published in 1801, and still in print up to 1914. Probably the most successful English text-book, it is best known in the Kate Greenaway edition. It had the same format as Vyse, but its contents were more acceptable to children. See page 19.

A Summary Method of Teaching Children to Read: an early attempt at a phonic method, an adaption of a French book, first published as *'Syllabic Spelling'*. This is a composite page of illustrations from Plates 2, 3 and 5. See page 33.

Carpenter's *Spelling Assistant* was not the traditional type of Speller, but one designed to teach spelling. It was frequently used in schools when words had to be spelled out and read individually before reading for meaning began. See page 32.

M'Culloch's *First Reading-Book* was a simplified version of the traditional Spellers, with some phonic elements, ending at simple reading lessons. It was cheap and was listed in the 1847 schedules which provided school managers with titles of approved school-books which could be bought at a discount. See page 28.

Reading Without Tears. Although there were phonic elements in the old Spellers and several attempts to introduce phonic methods — notably by the staff of Battersea Training College after 1840 — phonic methods were not widely accepted until *Reading Without Tears* appeared at the end of the period under review. In two volumes, well thought-out and well-designed, it was welcomed by Victorian governesses and was still in print in the 1930's. See page 34.

*Some Easy Lessons, co. sisting of Words not
exceeding Thee Letters.*

God is the God of all men: no one is as
he is. The way of man is ill; but not the
way of God. My son, do not lie; but try
to go in the way of God.

Do not sin; but try to use the way of
God. Go not in a bad way, nor put off the
law of God. All who sin go in a bad way.
Do you no ill, nor use the ill way; for the
end of it is bad.

My son, let not a bad boy sit by you;
nor go in his ill way if you are bid. For if
you do ill, you can not go to God. In God
do I put my joy, and to him do I cry all
the day.

My joy is to try the law of my God, and
not go in the way of sin; for if I do sin, I
can not go to God. Go not far from me, O
my God; and let me not go out of the way
of thy law.

If sin be in us, we are in an ill way. Let
us all go out of it; for it is bad for us. Who
can say, he has no sin, and is in the way of
God? Not one can say so. But all my joy
is to try and use the way of my God; for
no one is set far off by him, who is in his
way: but sin is our foe.

14 VYSE'S NEW LONDON SPELLING-BOOK.

The eye of God is on all men. In God
do I put my joy, and to him do I cry all
the day. If any man do ill, he can not go
to God; for the way of God is no ill way.
My son, do as you are bid; but if you are
bid do no ill.

I see thy way, O God; O how I joy in
it! O let me not sin! Let not my sin put
me off; let me not go to the pit; but try
me in thy way. The bad man is a foe to
God; and God is a foe to the bad man: so
let us not do ill.

---

*Easy Lessons, Consisting of Words not exceeding
Four Letters.*

I will mind thee, O Lord; for thou art
kind to me. Day by day will I pray to
thee. Go not far from me, O God, my God.
Keep me, O Lord, from such as love not
thy law and walk not in thy ways.

My son, if your ways are bad, see that
you mend; and the Lord will help you.
For the eye of the Lord is on all men; and
he will help all who cry to him.

I will mind the way of the Lord my God,
that I may not sin. I will shun them that
will hurt me, lest I be hurt by them. I
will not walk with them that are bad, lest I
be so too. But I will walk in the way of
my God, and then he will help me.

nui-sance	oint-ment	o-ver	pa-gan
num-ber	old-er	out-cast	pain-ful
nur-ture	ol-ive	out-cry	paint-er
nut-meg	o-men	out-most	paint-ing
Oaf-ish	on-set	out-side	pal-ace
ob-ject	o-pen	out-ward	pal-ate
ob-long	op-tic	out-works	pale-ness
o-dour	o-ral	ox-en	pal-let
of-fal	or-ange	Pack-age	pan-cake
of-fer	or-chard	pad-dle	pan-try
of-fice	or-gan	pad-dock	pa-per
o-gle	or-phan	pad-lock	pa-pist

Easy Lessons, continued.

O Lord, think not on the sins of my youth; but think on me, O Lord, for my good. All the paths of the Lord are truth to such as keep his laws. What man is he who fears the Lord; him shall he teach in the way he shall choose.

His soul shall dwell at ease, and his seed shall in-her-it the land. The Lord is my light and my health; whom then shall I fear? The Lord is the strength of my life; whom then shall I dread? When bad men, who are my foes, came home to de-stroy me, they fell down.

Though a host of men were laid to catch me, yet shall not my heart fear; and though they raise war up a-gainst me, yet will I put my trust in him. Set up thy-self; O God, a-bove the hea-vens, and thy glo-ry a-bove the earth.

Hear my voice, O Lord, when I cry to thee; O hide not thy face from me. Thou hast been my help: leave me not, nor go from me; for thou, O God, art my God; ear-ly will I seek thee

When my friends leave me, my God takes care of me. Give me not up to the will of my foes; for such as speak wrong rise up to do me hurt. I should faint, but that I think of thy love, O God, and live.

I will praise thee, O Lord: for thou hast set me up, and not made my foes to tri-umph o-ver me. O Lord, my God, I did cry un-to thee, and thou didst hear me. Thou, Lord, hast brought my soul out of hell: thou hast kept my life from them who go down in-to the pit.

Two Syllables, continued.

Par-boil	par-rot	pa-tron	pen-ny
par-cel	par-ry	pat-tern	pen-sive
parch-ment	par-son	pave-ment	pelt-ing
par-don	part-ner	pay-ment	pen-ance
pa-rents	pas-chal	pea-cock	pen-dant
par-ish	pas-sage	peb-ble	pen-man
par-ley	pas-sive	ped-lar	pep-per
par-lour	pa-tent	peep-er	per-fect

60

92   VYSE'S NEW LONDON SPELLING-BOOK.

who was killed by a serpent thirty feet long, and as thick as a man's body. It seized the poor man by the waist, and coiled itself round his head, neck, breast, and thighs, instantly crushing him to death. This serpent reduces its prey to one uniform mass, by crushing it with its spiral folds; it then lubricates the body with some mucilaginous substance, and distending its jaws, swallows it by one gradual and long-continued effort. When a stag has formed its meal, the horns, which it cannot swallow, are seen sticking out of its mouth. It is then easily destroyed, as it remains for a length of time stupid and unwieldy, till the process of digestion is over, when it again issues forth from its retreat, to the terror of all the animals of the forest. The bite of this snake is not venomous.

THE KANGUROO.

It is a native of New-Holland, where it was first discovered by Sir Joseph Banks.— Its head is small and taper, ears large and erect, upper lip divided, the end of the nose black, nostrils wide, lower jaw shorter than the upper, and there are whiskers on both; it also has strong hairs above and below the eyes ; its head, neck, and shoulders are small; the lower parts of the body increasing in thickness to the rump; its tail is long, very thick near the rump, and taper; its fore feet are extremely short, and are mostly used in digging or bringing its food to its mouth; it moves altogether on its hind legs, making successive bounds of ten or twelve feet, with such rapidity, as to outstrip the fleetest greyhound; it springs from rock to rock, and leaps over bushes seven or eight feet high, with great ease; it has five toes on its fore feet—three on the hind, the middle one very long; the inner claw is divided down the middle into two parts. The Kanguroo rests on its hind legs, which are hard, black, and naked on the under side. Its fur is short and soft, of a reddish ash colour, lighter on the lower parts.

THE ZEBRA.

The Zebra is at once one of the most elegant and the most untameable of animals. Its skin is as smooth as satin, and adorned with elegant stripes, like ribbons, which are brown on a yellowish white ground in the male, and in the female are black on a white ground. The body is round and plump, and the legs of a delicate smallness. The voice of this creature is thought to have a distant resemblance to the sound of a post-horn. The Zebra is chiefly found in the southern parts of Africa; whole herds are often seen grazing in those extensive plains that lie near the Cape of Good Hope

Historians say, that the bare aspect of this prince drew respect and veneration. He was gentle and beneficent to persons of virtue, but to the vicious, inexorable; a friend to the poor, the widow, and the orphan, and, indeed, to the unfortunate in general; his greatest delight being to soothe the misfortunes of mankind. His valour was well known to the world, but it never puffed him up. His subjects were also very dear to him; and the uninterrupted harmony that subsisted between him and his queen, augmented his felicity.

He died on the 21st day of June, 1377, in the 65th year of his age, and the 51st of his reign.

in 1377; and, 24 days after Edward's death, was crowned at Westminster, in the 19th year of his age.

He was son to Edward the Black Prince (so called on account of his wearing black armour, who was the first created prince of Wales.

This unfortunate prince, on his return from Ireland, was imprisoned in Flint Castle, but some time after was sent to Pontefract Castle, where Sir Piers Exton, with eight other men, was sent to destroy him. The king, however, resolved to sell his life as dear as possible, and killed four of the assassins before he fell himself, which happened by the hands of Exton. Thus died this unhappy prince, at 33 years of age.

HOUSE OF LANCASTER.

HENRY IV. SURNAMED BOLINGBROKE

This prince began his reign on the 29th of September, 1399 He was son to John of Gaunt, third son of Edward III.

His chief character was an extreme desire of reigning; and he came to the throne by a method that was universally disapproved, having caused Richard II. to be murdered, which will be an eternal blot on his memory.

He performed very few actions which merit any encomium; and his reign was a continued series or revolutions. It is said that he died of a leprosy, on the 20th of March, 1413, being the 14th year of his

RICHARD II.

This prince, who was grandson to the deceased king, was born at Bordeaux, on the 6th day of January 1366, and made prince of Wales

THE

ENGLISH SPELLING-BOOK,

ACCOMPANIED BY

A PROGRESSIVE SERIES

OF

Easy and Familiar Lessons,

INTENDED AS

AN INTRODUCTION

TO

THE ENGLISH LANGUAGE.

By WILLIAM MAVOR, LL. D.

Two Hundred and Seventy-seventh Edition, Revised and Improved.

LONDON:

PRINTED FOR LONGMAN, HURST, REES, ORME, AND BROWN,
PATERNOSTER-ROW; AND TO BE HAD OF ALL BOOKSELLERS IN TOWN
AND COUNTRY.

With a full and liberal allowance to Schools.

PRICE EIGHTEENPENCE, BOUND.

1822.

4   *The English Alphabet.*

A a   B b   C c

Ape   Bell   Cock

D d   E e   F f

Dog   Ea-gle   Fox

G g   H h   I i

Goose   Horse   Ink-stand

The *English Alphabet.* 5

J j   K k   L l

Jug   Kite   Li-on

M m   N n   O o

Mouse   Nut   Owl

P p   Q q   R r

Pig   Queen   Rab-bit

A 3

Lessons of ONE *Syllable.*

Lesson 11.

Try to learn fast. Thank those who teach you. Strive to speak plain. Speak as if the words were your own. Do not bawl; nor yet speak in too low a voice. Speak so that all in the room may hear you. Read as you talk.

Lesson 12.

Look! there is our dog Tray. He takes good care of the house. He will bark, but he will not bite if you do not hurt him.

Here is a fine sleek cat. She purs and frisks, and wags her tail. Do not teaze her, or she will scratch you, and make you bleed.

See what a sweet bird this is. Look at his bright eyes, his fine wings, and nice long tail.

Lesson 13.

Miss May makes all her friends laugh at her; if a poor mouse runs by her she screams for an hour; and a bee on her frock will put her in a fit; if a small fly should get on her hair and buz in her ear, she would call all in the house to help her as if she was hurt.

Lesson 14.

You must not hurt live things. You should not kill poor flies, nor pull off their legs nor wings. You must not hurt bees, for they do good, and will not sting you if you do not touch them. All things that have life can feel as well as you can.

66

84 *Lessons in Natural History.*

10. THE LION.

THIS noble animal has a large head, short round ears, a shaggy mane, strong limbs, and a long tail tufted at the ex-trem-i-ty. His general colour is tawny, which on the belly inclines to white. From the nose to the tail a full-grown lion will measure eight feet. The lioness is somewhat smaller, and destitute of a mane.

Like other animals, the lion is affected by the influence of climate in a very sensible degree. Under the scorching sun of Africa, where his courage is excited by the heat, he is the most terrible and undaunted of all quadrupeds.

A single lion of the desert will often rush upon a whole caravan, and face his enemies, in-sen-si-ble of fear, to the last gasp. To his keeper he appears to possess no small degree of attachment; and though his passions are strong, and his appetites vehement, he has been tried, and found to be noble in his resentment, mag-nan-i-mous in his courage, and grateful in his dis-po-si-ti-on. His roaring is so loud, that it pierces the ear like thunder.

67

11. THE ELEPHANT.

THE elephant is not only the largest, but the strongest of all quadrupeds; in a state of nature it is neither fierce nor mischievous. Pacific, mild, and brave, it only exerts its powers in its own defence, or in that of the com-mu ni-ty to which it belongs. It is social and friendly with its kind; the oldest of the troop always appears as the leader, and the next in se-ni-or-i-ty brings up the rear. As they march, the forest seems to tremble beneath them; in their passage they bear down the branches of trees, on which they feed; and if they enter cul-ti-va-ted fields, the labours of ag-ri-cul-ture soon disappear.

When the elephant is once tamed, it is the most gentle and o-be-di-ent of all animals. Its attachment to its keeper is re-mark-a-ble, and it seems to live but to serve and obey him. It is quickly taught to kneel in order to receive its rider; and it caresses those with whom it is acquainted.

V. THE KID AND THE WOLF

A She-Goat shut up her Kid in safety at home, while she went to feed in the fields, and advised her to keep close. A wolf watching their motions as soon as the Dam was gone, hastened to the house, and knocked at the door. Child, said he, counterfeiting the voice of the Goat, I forgot to embrace you; open the door, I beseech you, that I may give you this token of my affection. No! no! replied the Kid (who had taken a survey of the deceiver through the window), I cannot possibly give you admission; for though you feign very well the voice of my Dam, I perceive in every other respect that you are a Wolf.

> Let every youth, with cautious breast,
>   Allurement's fatal dangers shun,
> Who turns sage counsel to a jest,
>   Takes the sure road to be undone.
> A Parent's counsels e'er revere,
> And mingle confidence with fear.

E

A Summary Method of Teaching Children to Read

THE SCHOLAR'S

SPELLING ASSISTANT;

WHEREIN

THE WORDS

ARE ARRANGED ON AN IMPROVED PLAN,

According to their respective Principles of Accentuation ;

In a Manner calculated to familiarize the Art of Spelling and Pronunciation, to remove Difficulties, and to facilitate general Improvement.

INTENDED FOR

THE USE OF SCHOOLS AND PRIVATE TUITION.

BY THOMAS CARPENTER,

AUTHOR OF THE ENGLISH VOCABULARY, (DESIGNED AS A SEQUEL TO THE SPELLING ASSISTANT,) THE NEW ORTHOGRAPHICAL ASSISTANT, ETC.

A New Edition, corrected throughout.

LONDON:

PRINTED FOR

LONGMAN, BROWN, GREEN, AND LONGMANS;

AND

WHITTAKER AND CO

1843.

[*Price* 1s. 6d]

71

s. Gilt, *gilded*
s. Guilt, *sin*

s. Glaire, *white of an egg*
s. Glare, *a bright light*

s. Grate, *fire place*
s. Great, *large*

s. Grôan, *a deep sigh*
part. Grown, *increased*

s. Hail, *frozen rain*
s. Hale, *strong, robust*

s. Hair, *of the head*
s. Hare, *an animal*

s. Hall, *a large room*
v. Haul, *to pull about*

s. Hart, *an animal*
s. Heart, *the seat of life*

v. Heal, *to cure*
s. Heel, *of the foot or shoe*

v. Hear, *to hearken*
ad. Here, *in this place*

part. Heard, *of the verb* to hear
s. Herd, *a drove*

v. Hew, *to cut*
s. Hue, *shade of colour*
s. Hugh, *a man's name*

pro. Him, *that man*
s. Hymn, *a holy song*

s. Hole, *a cavity*
a. Whole, *entire*

s. Hoop, *for a cask*
v. Whoop, *to shout*

pro. I, *myself*
s. Eye, *the organ of sight*

s. { Ile, / Aisle, } *of a church*
s. Isle, *an island*

prep. In, *within*
s. Inn, *a public house*

s. Key, *for a lock*
s. Quay, *a wharf*

v. Kill, *to deprive of life*
s. Kiln, *for drying corn*

s. Knap, *the down on cloth*
s. Nap, *short sleep*

s. Knave, *a rogue*
s. Nave, *of a wheel*

v. Knead, *to work dough*
s. Need, *poverty*

v. Knew, *did know*
a. New, *fresh, modern*

s. Knight, *a title of honour*
s. Night, *time of darkness*

v. Know, *to understand*
ad. No, *not so*

v. Know²s, *he knoweth*
s. No²se, *of the face*

FIRST READING-BOOK

FOR

THE USE OF SCHOOLS;

CONTAINING

THE ALPHABET, AND PROGRESSIVE LESSONS ON THE LONG
AND SHORT SOUNDS OF THE VOWELS.

BY

J. M. M'CULLOCH, D. D.,

Formerly Head-Master of Circus-Place School, Edinburgh ; Author of
" A Manual of English Grammar, Philosophical and Practical," &c.

Sixteenth Edition.

―――――――

EDINBURGH :

OLIVER & BOYD, TWEEDDALE COURT.

LONDON : SIMPKIN, MARSHALL, & CO.

―――

MDCCCLII.

7

THE ALPHABET.

a b c d e f g

h i j k l m n o

p q r s t u v

w x y z

A B C D E F G H I J

K L M N O P Q R S

T U V W X Y Z

---

b d, c e, h k, m w, n u, p q, s z

VOWELS.

a e i o u w y

CONSONANTS.

b c d f g h j k l m n

p q r s t v w x y z

COMPOUND CONSONANTS.

ch sh th

8

LONG VOWELS WITH AN INITIAL CONSONANT.

a   e   i   o   u   y—b   p   f   v

SYLLABLES.

ba	be	bi	bo	bu	by
pa	pe	pi	po	pu	py
fa	fe	fi	fo	fu	fy
va	ve	vi	vo	vu	vy

d   t   s   z

da	de	di	do	du	dy
ta	te	ti	to	tu	ty
sa	se	si	so	su	sy
za	ze	zi	zo	zu	zy

l   m   n   r

la	le	li	lo	lu	ly
ma	me	mi	mo	mu	my
na	ne	ni	no	nu	ny
ra	re	ri	ro	ru	ry

c   g   h   j   k   w   y

ce	ci	ga	ge	go	gu
ha	he	hi	ho	hu	hy
ja	je	ji	jo	ju	
ka	ke	ki	ko	ku	
wa	we	wi	wo	ye	yo

9

sh ch th*

sha	she	shi	sho	shu	shy
cha	che	chi	cho	chu	chy
tha	the	thi	tho	thu	thy

WORDS.

be	mè	he		po	so	⁻lo	
we	ye	she		no	ho	go	wo
the	by	fy		de-fy	re-ly		
my	shy	thy		ty-ro	he-ro		

SENTENCES.

No, o no.
O fy!
Be by.
Be by me.
Go by.
Go by me.
We go.
Lo! we go.
So I go.
So we go.
No, go ye.
Ye go by me.

Ho, ye go by me.
O no.
Be ye so?
Ye de-fy me.
He a he-ro! po.
We re-ly.
A ty-ro.
The he-ro.
Be shy! no.
My wo.
Thy wo.
Be she so.

---

* As these combined consonants express simple sounds, and
are designed to supply a defect in the *letters* of the Alphabet,
they should be considered as *single* consonants, and pronounced
by the pupil in such a manner as to exhibit their true character
and simple sound.

A 2

10

SHORT VOWELS FOLLOWED BY A CONSONANT.

SYLLABLES.

ab	eb	ib	ob	ub
ap	ep	ip	op	up
af	ef	if	of	uf
av	ev	iv	ov	uv
ad	ed	id	od	ud
at	et	it	ot	ut
as	es	is	os	us
az	ez	iz	oz	uz
al	el	il	ol	ul
am	em	im	om	um
an	en	in	on	un
ar*	er	ir	or	ur
ag	eg	ig	og	ug
ak	ek	ik	ok	uk
ax	ex	ix	ox	ux
ash	esh	ish	osh	ush
ach	ech	ich	och	uch
ath	eth	ith	oth	uth

WORDS.

at	am	an	ash	on	or	ox
if	it	in		up	up-on	us

* Though *ar*, *er*, &c. are here classed with *an*, *en*, &c., the vowels followed by *r* are not to be pronounced like the vowels followed by *l*, *m*, &c., but with that modification which the letter *r* always imparts to a preceding vowel.

11

SENTENCES.

In it.	It is* in.
Up at it.	It is up.
Up at us.	It is an ox.
On us.	It is up-on an ox.
An ox.	It is as* it is.
On an ox.	It is an ash.
I am on an ox.	Is it g or j ?
Up on it.	It is j, is it ?
On, up-on an ox.	Is it on, or up-on ?

LONG and SHORT VOWELS PROMISCUOUSLY.

SYLLABLES.

ba	ab	fe	ef
fa	af	ra	ar
da	ad	pa	ap
su	us	vi	iv
la	al	se	es
ne	en	mi	im
bi	ib	ga	ag

WORDS.

no   on.   ho   oh.

po-et	po-em	li-on
di-et	fu-el	li-ar
ri-ot	di-al	vi-ol
su-et	vi-al	du-el

---

* The child should be told that *s* sounds like *z* in *is*, *his*, *as*, and *has*.

78

Facsimile Pages

12

SENTENCES.

It is he.
It is my ox.
We go in.
Ye go in.
I am on an ox.
Is he up or no?
We go as ye go.
Lo! I am up.
I go on my ox.
Is it a vi-al or a vi-ol?

A po-em is by a po-et.
He is a li-ar.
It is a li-on.
O fy, a ri-ot!
No su-et is in my di-et.
Lo, a di-al!
He is no he-ro, if he is in a du-el.
Oh, she is so shy!

WORDS OF TWO LETTERS SOUNDED
IRREGULARLY.

do   to   of*.

Do so.
Wo to me.
We go, do ye go?
Is he to go on the ox?
He is to do it.
Is it if or of?

O fy, to ri-ot so!
Wo be to us, if we do as ye do.
The di-al is of ash.
Is it the ox or the li-on?

* The pupil, at this stage of his progress, may be taught to pronounce these words without spelling them, in the same way as he is taught the letters of the Alphabet.

13

SHORT VOWELS PRECEDED AND FOLLOWED BY A CONSONANT.

WORDS.

bad	fat	sat	man	had
bat	fan	lap	nag	hat
bag	vat	lad	rat	ham
pad	van	map	ram	Sam
pat	Dan	mad	ran	wag
pan	tax	mat	gat	wax

SENTENCES.

It is my bag.

He is a wag.

Is the pad on the nag?

A fat rat.

A fat ham in the bag.

Sam has a hat on.

He is a bad lad.

Dan has to pat the ram.

She sat on the mat; as the rat ran.

My hat is in the bag on my lap.

She has the fan in my bag.

I am to go in the van.

She had a fan.

I had a bag.

WORDS.

bed	vex	led	net	jet
pet	den	let	red	web
pen	ten	met	get	wet
fed	set	men	hen	yes

20

He is a dupe.
The duke is of wide fame.
Dive in the wave in June.
My pipe is mute.
The duke is on a mule.
The hum of the hive is mute.

WORDS.

ire*	hare	mere	bore	wore
ore	share	fire	tore	pure
dare	here	wire	more	sure

SENTENCES.

Men dig in a pit for ore—i-ron ore, tin ore, sil-ver ore.
I dare not take a hare, it is game.
Here is the share due to me.
A mere sot—it is a sin to be a sot.
I bake the tile in a fire.
My line is made of wire.
She bore the hive on a pole.
Bore a hole in the pole.
Let him take more time.
Dive in the pure wave in June.
She wore a nice lace robe.
I am sure he tore the lace robe.

---

* The child should be taught that the long vowels, when followed by *r*, have their sound lengthened and modified, as if by the addition of short *u*. Thus, *dare* is pronounced *da'-ŭr ; here, he'-ŭr*, &c.

21

LONG AND SHORT VOWELS WITH A CON-
SONANT PRECEDING AND FOLLOWING.

WORDS.

pat	pate	dam	dame	man	mane
pan	pane	lad	lade	rat	rate
fat	fate	mad	made	gat	gate
van	vane	mat	mate	hat	hate

SENTENCES.

Pat me on the pate.

Is it a pan or a pane on the fire?

The fat man met a sad fate.

Has a man a mane?

Men do not fix a vane on the top of a van.

Do not lade the lad so.

Is dam the same as dame?

Wine made the man mad.

Run, rat, at a fine rate.

He gat in at the gate.

I hate a hat made of fur.

The lad in the lane has tape to tie up
the mat.

WORDS.

bit	bite	din	dine	hid	hide
pin	pine	sit	site	kin	kine
fin	fine	rid	ride	win	wine

SENTENCES.

Bite a bit of bun.

This pin is made of pine.

Here is a fine fin.

22

Go to dine, but make no din.
Sit on the site of the hive.
If I get rid of it, I go to ride.
I hid my hat, let Tom hide his.
He ran a race to win a pipe of wine.

WORDS.

| mop | mope | rob | robe | rot | rote |
| not | note | rod | rode | hop | hope |

SENTENCES.

Use the mop, do not mope.
She has not a note of the tune.
Do not rob me of my robe.
The lad rode on a rod or pole.
Is it hop or hope?

WORDS.

tub tube   tun tune

SENTENCES.

A tube is not so big as a tub.
A tun of wine—a tune on the lute.
The bud of a tu-lip.
The rose has a fine per-fume.
Do not mope; I did it in pure fun.

LONG AND SHORT VOWELS IN WORDS WITH
FINAL s or 's.

WORDS.

| vats | apes | nags | makes | rags | gates |
| lad's | lanes | rats | waves | hats | hates |

23

pens	Eve's	pits	vines	dogs	ores
hens	cedes	sits	miles	robs	ropes

runs   duke's   pies   lies   toes

ti'-gers   li'-ars   met'-als
tu'-lips   li'-ons   fin'-gers

SENTENCES.

Dogs bite.
Men dig in pits for the ores of met-als.
The duke rides on a fine nag.
The hare runs in the lane.
Shut the gates.
Pa-per is made of lin-en rags.
He gave five pens for a pop-gun.
I like to dive in the pure waves.

The tu-lips bud in June.
It is nine miles to the duke's.
The duke's ape bit the man.
The bat sits in the shade in the lanes.
I get hot pies to din-ner.
Fix the ropes to the top of the pole.
Lies make a man a li-ar.
God hates li-ars.
Hens run be-fore a fox.
Dogs run af-ter a hare.

I met these lads in the lane.
This lad's hat is of chip.

READING WITHOUT TEARS. **21**

Note.— *Let the consonants be called as they are sounded, b′, c′, d′, &c. Let c have its hard sound, like* k.

a is like a goose on the water

b is like a child with a wide frock behind, coming to you

c is like an open mouth

l is like a candlestick with a bit at top broken off

m is like two dogs' kennels joined together

n is like a dog's kennel

o is like a small ball

82   READING WITHOUT TEARS.

Ape a   Baby b   Cup c   Doll d

Eagle e   Fox f   Gun g   Hat h   Iron i

Jar j   Kite k   Lamp l   Mouse m

Nut n   Oak o   Pin p   Quail q

Rod r   Saucer s   Table t   Unicorn u   Viper v

Wolf w   Express x   Youth y   Zigzag z

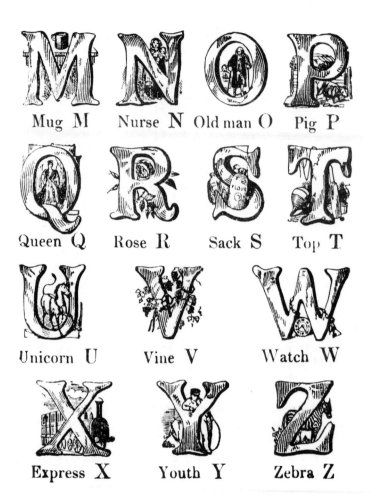

Mug M   Nurse N   Old man O   Pig P

Queen Q   Rose R   Sack S   Top T

Unicorn U   Vine V   Watch W

Express X   Youth Y   Zebra Z

Cap   Cab   Cat

CAP   CAB   CAT

cap   cab   cat

NOTE.—*Teachers are recommended to tell the Child the letters over and over again, and to help it to spell, as by this means it will find delight in its book.* The words must always be spelt, *for otherwise the Child would name the pictures without looking at the words.*

Hat Ham

HAT HAM

hat ham

NOTE.—*It is not advisable to keep to one page till it is known perfectly, but soon to pass on to another; thus enticing the child by novelty.*

Bed	Net	Leg	Den	Bell
fed	met	beg	hen	sell
led	get	keg	men	tell
red	wet	peg	ten	well

I had a red bed

I had a wet hen

I fed ten men in a den

I led ten men to a well

Note.—*Do not notice double letters, but say l' e l', as if there was only one* l. *Good spelling will be learned hereafter*

238 READING WITHOUT TEARS.

Rain	Gl ean	Vine	Stone	Tune
ain	ean	ine	one	une
tr ain	bean	mine	bone	
st ain	seen	line	moan	June
cr ane	mean	fine	groan	

I have a dog.   His name is Tr ay.
He can sw im well.
He will do as he is bid.

James dr op-ped his hat in the riv-er.

Tr ay seiz-ed it and laid it at the feet of James.   James pat-ted Tr ay on the back.

93

Tr ay nev-er bites, but he licks.

Tr ay has bl ack legs.

Tr ay has a bl ack sp ot on his back.

Tr ay has a fine bl ack tail.

Tr ay moans. Is he in pain? Yes.

Did you beat him? Yes, I did.

Tr ay st ole a bit of meat.

Fie, fie, my Tr ay. Nev-er st eal.

I do not like to beat you, but I like you to be-have well.

Tr ay will not st eal a-gain.

I will leave a bit of meat in his way, to see if he will take it.

No, he has not eat-en it.

Pat him and pr aise him.

Give Tr ay a bone to pick.

READERS— APPROVED OR POPULAR

The National Reader was a sequel to the National Spelling Book. Many Spellers had sequels which contained further selections of reading lessons, poems, Greek legends, short biographies, and other matters to improve the mind.

Peep of Day, by the author of *Reading Without Tears*, first published in 1833, sold 250,000 copies by 1867. Originally designed to be read to children, after the publication of *Reading Without Tears* it was listed as a follow-up reader, together with seven other similar books by the same author. Together they made a complete reading course 'to satisfy a child's requirements between the ages of four and twelve.'

The Child's Guide to Knowledge, by Mrs Ward. Small catechisms were popular during the first half of the century; Pinnock's are the best-known, but *The Child's Guide* was more substantial, more interesting, easier to read, and very popular with children.

The Child's Companion, published by the Religious Tract Society. A monthly periodical, price one penny, sold in Sunday Schools to combat the 'cheap Trash' that the children might otherwise buy.

Watt's *Divine and Moral Songs*. A Houlston example. To conteract the evil effects of stories of crime, horror and superstition, various organisations and firms saturated the country with their own tracts, chapbooks and magazines. Many remained in print to the end of the century as penny reward books.

Little George and his Penny, by Mrs. Sherwood. Another Houlston publication in the chapbook tradition. For examples of 'real' chapbooks, see Victor Neuburg's *'Penny Histories'*, O.U.P., 1968. Facsimiles of two of Mrs. Sherwood's books may be seen in *'Mrs. Sherwood and her Books for Children'*, by M. Nancy Cutt, O.U.P., 1974.

Beauty and the Beast. The heroes of the old chapbooks survived in a more respectable form. Oliver & Boyd, Dean & Munday, and other firms produced books which were more interesting to middle-class children than the moral tales of Mrs. Cameron and Mrs. Sherwood.

General Wolfe's Song. An example of a broadsheet (reduced) printed for the literate poor. For examples of ephemeral reading matter produced by the Catnach Press and others, see *'Curiosities of Street Literature'*, Broadsheet King, 1966.

170

CHAPTER XVIII.

———◆———

LESSON I.

THE CAMELEOPARD.

THIS singular animal is found in the remotest parts of Africa. It seems to partake of the nature of different quadrupeds. Its slender body bears some affinity to the camel and the stag; its head is not unlike that of the deer; it has two short horns, about six inches long, which it sheds every year; its neck resembles that of the horse; and the great length of its fore-legs over that of its hind ones, gives it, when standing, the attitude of a dog when sitting.

In the British Museum there is a skin of one of these animals stuffed. Its height to the top of its head is about twelve feet, though there are some eighteen feet high. Its colour is a beautiful brown, variegated with white spots.

The cameleopard lives wholly on vegetables; and, when grazing, is obliged to spread its fore-feet very wide, in order to reach the ground with its mouth.

No animal seems less calculated by nature for its own defence than the cameleopard; nor is there any less adapted to the use of man. In walking, the horse lifts his legs on one side, then on the other; in trotting, he lifts them diagonally; in galloping, he takes them up one by one; but the clumsy cameleopard, in galloping, moves its two legs on each side at the same time, and travels with so much pain, that it is soon fatigued. It is very timid, and consequently perfectly harmless.

LESSON V.

THE HOPPOE.

THE Hoppoe has a beautiful crest of black and yellow feathers, which he can raise or let fall at pleasure. In the middle of the tail is a white spot, like a new moon; the wings and tail are black, with bars of white; the legs are short, and the outer toe is partly fixed to the middle toe. Its common food is those insects that are found on or near the ground,—as beetles, ants, worms, dragon-flies, wild-bees, and caterpillars. He is fond of marshy places, where there are plenty of such insects. Like woodpeckers, they lay their eggs in the holes of trees. The Egyptians say, that the young hoppoes shew their affection to their parents when they are cold, by warming them under their wings.

When we contemplate the variety of the productions of Nature, and the ample provision made by its Author for all the animals which stock the well-replenished earth, our mind is naturally led to consider our Heavenly father's character, so beautifully set forth by Mrs. Barbauld.

> I READ God's awful name emblazon'd high
> With golden letters on the illumin'd sky;
> Nor less the mystic characters I see
> Wrought in each flow'r, inscrib'd on ev'ry tree;
> In ev'ry leaf that trembles to the breeze,
> I hear the voice of God among the trees.
> With thee in shady solitudes I walk,
> With thee in busy crowded cities talk;
> In every creature own thy forming power,
> In each event thy providence adore,
>
> Thy hopes shall animate my drooping soul,
> Thy precepts guide me, and thy fear control;
> Thus shall I rest, unmov'd by all alarms,
> Secure within the temple of thine arms;
> From anxious cares, from gloomy terrors free,
> And feel myself omnipotent in thee.

98

To face page 184.

THE COMMON HERON.

THE CUCKOO.

THE BUSTARD.

THE HOOPOE.

HUMMING BIRDS.

Peep of Day

speak, and she often kissed you, and called you sweet names.

Is your mother kind to you still? —Yes she is, though she is sometimes angry. But she wishes to make you good: that is why she is sometimes angry.

Your mother has sent you to this nice school, and she gives you supper when you go home. I know she will be kind to you as long as she lives.

But remember who gave you this mother. God sent you to a dear mother, instead of putting you in the fields, where no one would have seen you or taken care of you.

Can your mother keep you alive?— No.

She can feed you, but she cannot make your breath go on.

God thinks of you every moment.[4]

[4] "Are not five sparrows sold for two farthings, and not one of them is forgotten before God? But even the very hairs of your head are all numbered." Luke xii. 6, 7.

Peep of Day

THE CHILD'S

GUIDE TO KNOWLEDGE:

BEING A

COLLECTION OF USEFUL

AND FAMILIAR QUESTIONS AND ANSWERS ON

EVERY-DAY SUBJECTS,

𝕬𝖉𝖆𝖕𝖙𝖊𝖉 𝖋𝖔𝖗 𝖄𝖔𝖚𝖓𝖌 𝕻𝖊𝖗𝖘𝖔𝖓𝖘,

AND

ARRANGED IN THE MOST SIMPLE AND EASY LANGUAGE.

BY A LADY.

THIRTEENTH EDITION, GREATLY ENLARGED.

LONDON:

PUBLISHED BY SIMPKIN, MARSHALL, & Co.;

AND SOLD BY

HARVEY & DARTON; AND ALL BOOKSELLERS.

MDCCCXLIV.

Price Three Shillings.

said to be a study *too difficult for the mind of man*.

Q. What is tripoli?

A. A kind of clay of an earthy texture; formerly brought into Egypt from Tripoli, in Africa, but is now found in many parts of Germany.

Q. What is its use?

A. It is valued for the polishing of metals and stones, mixed with sulphur.

Q. Is not what we call rotten-stone a kind of tripoli?

A. Yes: it is dug in Derbyshire and Staffordshire, and is used for most of the purposes of tripoli.

Q. What is whitening?

A. A pounded chalk.

Q. What is putty?

A. It is made of white lead, whitening and oil, well mixed together.

Q. What are flints?

A. Hard stones, found in pieces of different sizes, and commonly among chalk.

Q. What are they principally useful for?

o 3

THE

CHILD'S COMPANION;

OR,

Sunday Scholar's Reward.

No. 36.]   DECEMBER, 1834.   [Vol. 3.

THE END OF THE YEAR.

My young readers; has another year indeed flown away? then are we so much
nearer the end of our pilgrimage; so much
nearer eternity.   Spring came with her fresh-
ening breezes and balmy showers, the birds
sang in the branches, and the tender buds put
forth their blossoms, ushering in gay summer,
decked with her fruits and flowers: autumn
followed, when the fields yielded their increase; God sent a plentiful harvest for

NEW SERIES.   N

352

HYMN FOR THE YOUNG.

Prov. viii. 32—36.

'Tis Wisdom calls aloud,
And bids the young draw near;
Let children now her temple crowd,
And her instructions hear.

" Hearken to me," she cries,
" Ye children, learn my ways;
From heaven I come, to make you wise,
And bless your earliest days.

" They shall be blest indeed,
Who keep my ways with care;
Who watch for me, with earnest heed,
And daily, fervent prayer.

" Yes, they shall Wisdom gain,
Who wait at Wisdom's door;
Grace of the Lord they shall obtain,
And life for evermore."

Wisdom and Christ are one;
All who his grace abuse,
Wrong their own soul, and madly run
To meet the death they choose.

Essex.   J. B.

Printed for the Religious Tract Society, Paternoster-row; by J. Hill, Black-horse-court, Fleet-st.

DIVINE SONGS.

GLORY TO THE FATHER, AND THE SON,
AND THE HOLY SPIRIT.

TO God the Father, God the Son,
  And God the Spirit, Three in One,
Be honour, praise, and glory given,
By all on earth, and all in heaven.

NOW let the Father, and the Son,
  And Spirit be ador'd,
Where there are works to make him known,
  Or saints to love the Lord.

GIVE to the Father praise,
  Give glory to the Son ;
And to the Spirit of his grace
  Be equal honour done.

106

MORAL SONGS.

1. THE SLUGGARD.

'TIS the voice of the sluggard ; I heard
    him complain,
"You have wak'd me too soon, I must
    slumber again."
As the door on its hinges, so he on his bed,
Turns his sides, and his shoulders, and his
    heavy head.

14   LITTLE GEORGE

" Spend that well, my boy, and you shall have half-a-crown to-morrow."

So little George thanked his grand father, and kissed him, and ran with his penny into the street, saying, " Shall I buy a cake, or a ball of string, or some gingerbread, or some sugar-candy, or a horse, or a cart, or a penny knife?   But I will not buy any thing to eat, because I was sick yesterday, and perhaps I might get something which might make me sick to-day.   I will buy a knife."

Then little George went from shop to shop, to get a knife for his penny; and, at last, a shopkeeper let him have one.

Then little George was much pleas-
ed, for he had never had a knife before; and he ran home, to look for a
stick in the garden, to cut with his
new knife.　He soon found a stick,
and began to cut it;　but while he
was cutting with all his strength, for
the knife was blunt, his hand slipped,
and he cut himself very much.　Poor

The Merchant imploring the Beast to pardon him.

page 13

Beauty's offer to die, to save her Father's life

page 16

BEAUTY

AND

THE BEAST;

OR, THE

MAGIC ROSE.

WITH ELEGANT COLOURED ENGRAVINGS.

———

A NEW EDITION,
REVISED, AND ADAPTED FOR JUVENILE READERS,
BY A LADY.

———

London:

DEAN AND MUNDAY, THREADNEEDLE STREET.

BEAUTY AND THE BEAST.

There was once a rich merchant who had six children, three boys and three girls. The daughters were all handsome, but particularly the youngest; so very beautiful indeed was she, that every one called her Little Beauty, and when she was grown up, nobody called her by any other name, which made her sisters extremely jealous.

This youngest sister was not only handsomer than her sisters, but was also better tempered: the two eldest were extremely proud of being rich,

2

GENERAL
Wolfe's Song.

J. & T. Sweet, Printers, Strood.

HOW stands the glass around?
For shame! ye take no care, my boys!
How stands the glass around?
Let mirth and wine abound.
The trumpets sound,
The colours they are flying, boys,
To fight, kill, or wound;
May we still be found
Content with our hard fate, my boys,
On the cold ground.

Why, soldiers, why
Should we be melancholy, boys!
Why, soldiers, why,
Whose business 'tis to die?
What—sighing? fie!
Don't fear, drink on, be jolly, boys;
'Tis he, you, or I,—
Cold, hot, wet, or dry,
We're always found to follow, boys,
And scorn to fly.

'Tis but in vain,
I mean not to upbraid you, boys,
'Tis but in vain
For soldiers to complain:
Should next campaign
Send us to Him who made us, boys,
We're free from pain;
But if we remain,
A bottle and kind landlady
Cure all again.

APPENDIX A
BOOKS WHICH WERE USED
FOR THE TEACHING OF READING

This list includes alphabet books, primers, spellers and first readers; in fact, any book which was designed to be used for the teaching of reading, and many which were not, but are known to have been in use. It includes many books published before 1800, either because they continued in use after that date, or because they were influential or are mentioned in the text.

Books which I have been unable to find in any collection, but which are to be found in the London Catalogue of Books are listed with (Lond. Cat.) after the name of the publisher. Dates of first editions are given in brackets if they are known to differ from the dates of the editions listed.

The books are listed alphabetically by author, or by title if anonymous, and an index of titles is given at the end.

Although I have not included books in which the main aim was the improvement of morals, the tiles of many others are missing; many have not survived, like that of Dr. Johnson's English Master, Tom Brown, who "published a spelling-book, and dedicated it to the Universe; but, I fear, no copy of it can now be had."

If any reader has in his possession a book, the title of which he feels should have been included, I would be grateful if he would let me know, so that it can be entered in a later edition.

Abbot, A.
THE MOTHER'S PRIMER, or first book for children
Edinburgh, Oliver & Boyd, (c.1825).

Abbot, Gorham Dummer.
ENGLISH SPELLING BOOK. Taylor & Walton. (Lond.
Cat.)
FIRST ENGLISH READER. Taylor & Walton. (Lond.
Cat.)
SECOND ENGLISH READER. Taylor & Walton. (Lond.
Cat.)

ABC FOR THE NURSERY. (c.1840)
With 26 coloured woodcuts.

THE ALBION PRIMER, or first book for children.
Fairburn, (c.1815)

ALDERMAN'S FEAST; a new alphabet. Dean & Co.,
(c.1845).

Alderson, James.
ORTHOGRAPHICAL EXERCISES: in a series of moral
letters. (1793). 5th. ed., with additions, J. Scatchard,
(c.1798). 14th. ed., rev. and corr. by Rev. Thos. Smith;
Law & Whittaker, etc., 1818.

ALDIBORONTOPHOSKYPHORNIOSTIKOS. Dean & Co.,
(c.1820).
An 'entertaining' alphabet derived from Arabian Nights.

THE ALPHABET. Aberdare, J.T.Jones, (c.1800).
A Battledore.

(ALPHABET, a coloured pictorial.) (c.1810).
*Engraved throughout; coloured frontis., 26 coloured plates
of alphabet, 8 coloured plates of story about apprentice.*

(ALPHABET, an alliterative, in panoramic form.) (c.1850).

(ALPHABET, illustrated with engravings of animals.)
(c.1800).

THE ALPHABET DISPLAYED BY SENSIBLE
OBJECTS. Newbery, (c.1760).
*Illustrated alphabet; 'The ravens caw Aa.' Each letter
with its picture is engraved.*

THE ALPHABET ILLUSTRATED. Glasgow, 1848.

THE ALPHABET IN VERSE. Newbery, (c.1760).
*Illustrated alphabet; 'Here comes A with an Apple you
see.' Each letter has a wood-cut.*

THE ALPHABET IN VERSE. Darton & Harvey, 1800.

THE ALPHABET LEARNED IN THE ROYAL NURSERY. 1845.

THE ALPHABET OF COMMON OBJECTS. Darton & Clark, (c.1849).

THE ALPHABET OF EXCITEMENT. Harwood, (c.1840). *Subjects are depicted in the shape of letters. Lithographic plates.*

ALPHABET OF FEMALE COSTUME. (c.1830). *26 cards. Each has hand-coloured lithograph of costume from a different country.*

THE ALPHABET OF GOODY TWO SHOES. I. Harris, 1808.

THE ALPHABET OF GOODY TWO SHOES. By learning which she soon got rich. Harris, (c.1832).

THE ALPHABET OF GOODY TWO SHOES; with spelling and reading lessons. Grant & Griffith, (c.1845).

ALPHABET OF QUADRUPEDS. Blair (c.1840). *Home Treasury Series, ed. by Felix Summerly. 3/-, or 5/- coloured.*

ALPHABETS AND PICTURES FOR CHILDREN, etc. W. Darton, (c.1824.

THE AMUSING ALPHABET FOR YOUNG CHILDREN BEGINNING TO READ. Taylor, 1812. *With 25 full-page engravings, and a story for each letter of the alphabet.*

AMUSING ALPHABET, or easy steps to ABC. Dean & Co., 1841.

THE AMUSING ALPHABET; to which is added the rise, progress and reward of industry. Oliver & Boyd, (c.1830). *One of a series of Oliver & Boyd Juvenile Books.*

AMUSING OBSERVATIONS PURPOSED TO BE MADE BY CHILDREN IN EARLY LIFE, WHICH WILL ENABLE THEM TO READ . . . . by the author of . . . . 'Summer Rambles', etc. Harris, 1808. *One of the earliest illustrated 'first readers' where the pictures really suit the text.*

THE ANTI-SPELLING BOOK; a new system of teaching children to read without spelling. Bull & Churton, 1833.

Arnold, Thomas Kerchever.
SPELLING TURNED ETYMOLOGY. Part 1. Rivington
1844.
*Preface: My object in this work is to enable even a village
schoolmaster to train his pupils to a considerable knowledge of words . . . . I feel convinced that, by frequent
repetition, even village children may acquire an extensive
vocabulary, and be taught to use it accurately.*

THE ART OF TEACHING IN SPORT; designed as a
prelude to a set of toys, for enabling ladies to instill the
rudiments of spelling, reading, grammar, and arithmetic,
under the idea of amusement. J. Marshall, (c.1770). 1785.
*Later called THE FRIEND OF MOTHERS. Attributed
by Mrs. Trimmer to Lady Fenn.*

(Atkins, Sarah)
THE JUVENILE RAMBLER, in a series of easy reading
lessons, designed for children, by the author of 'Grove
Cottage'. (c.1827).

AUNT ANN'S LESSON BOOK, for very young children, in
words of one and two syllables. Harvey & Darton, 1822.

THE AUNT'S GIFT, a new battledoor. Darton & Harvey,
1795.

BABY TALES; or easy lessons for infant minds. New ed.,
Wallis, (c.1825).
Two alphabets, word lists and anecdotes.

Barbauld, Anna Laetitia (Aikin).
LESSONS FOR CHILDREN, from two to three years old.
(1778). 1788. J. Johnson, 1794; 1797; 1812. Corr. and imp.,
Darton & Son, (c.1835). Enl., rev., in 4 parts, J. F. Dove,
(c.1830). In 4 parts, (Part 4; for children from three to four
years old), Baldwin, Cradock & Joy, 1818-20; 1821-25.
Edinburgh, Nelson, 1840. Darton & Clark, 1843. New ed.,
Longman, etc., 1851. Scott Webster & Geary, 1843.
*The author had been unable to find a book written in
words that children could understand, printed on good
paper in large type with wide spaces between the lines.
The book was criticised by the Edgeworths, but was
extremely popular. Mrs Trimmer thought that it gave a
new turn to the composition and mode of printing books
for little children. It inspired her 'Little Spelling Book.'*

Barwell, Louisa Mary (Bacon).
LITTLE LESSONS FOR LITTLE LEARNERS, in words
of one syllable.
Westley & Davis, 1833. J. Harris, 1838. Darton & Co., 1850.
Anticipated modern educational views. 14 edns.

(Battledore, untitled). E. Billing, (c.1830).

(Battledore, untitled) printed by Dean & Munday.
Cuts on outer: The Tame Rabbit, The Pig.

(Battledores, untitled) printed by R. Harrild, 20 Great East-
cheap, (c.1825). Designated by title of woodcut on middle
panel on outer:
a) The Fallow Deer.
b) The Cock.

(Battledores, untitled) printed by J. G. Rusher, Banbury,
although not all bear this imprint. Designated by title of
woodcut on middle panel on outer:
a) Playing with Fire.
b) The Camel.
c) The Lion.
d) Elephant and Child.
e) Arab and his Horse.
f) Chairs to Mend.
g) Young Lambs to Sell.
h) Monkey Turned Cook.
i) Teazing the Ass.

(Battledores, untitled) printed by Salter, Welshpool, (c.1825)
Designated by title of woodcut on middle panel on outer:
a) The Panther, The Ass.
b) The Ship, The Elephant.
c) The Buck, The Cascade.
d) Horses, The Tiger.
e) The Elephant, King's Arms.
f) The Lion, The Bear.

(Battledore, untitled) printed by C. N. Wright, Nottingham,
(c.1830).

BATTLEDORE, 1. No imprint, (c.1840).

Bearcroft, William.
PRACTICAL ORTHOGRAPHY; or, the art of teaching
spelling by writing; containing an improved method of
dictating, with exercises for practice; and collections of
words of difficult, irregular, and variable spelling.
Longman, etc., (c.1824).

Bentley, Hugh.
BRITISH CLASS BOOK, PROSE AND VERSE.
Cradock. (Lond. Cat.).

Berthaud (Sieur) see Williams, H. M.

BERTIE'S INDESTRUCTABLE WORD BOOK. Bogue,
(c.1850).
Printed on linen.

Bewick, Thomas.
A NEW LOTTERY BOOK OF BIRDS AND BEASTS,
FOR CHILDREN TO LEARN THEIR LETTERS AS
SOON AS THEY CAN SPEAK. Newcastle, T. Saint,
1771. Newcastle, Charnley, 1771.

Bigland, John.
THE NEW PRONOUNCING AND SPELLING BOOK,
accompanied by a series of instructive and interesting
lessons. 5th. ed., Derby, Mozley, (c.1824). 8th. ed., (c.1835)

Birkin, William.
THE RATIONAL ENGLISH EXPOSITOR AND
GUIDE TO PRONUNCIATION. Derby, Mozley & Sons,
1838.

Bishop, James.
THE CHILD'S NEW BOOK OF EASY TALES, in words
of one or two syllables. Dean & Munday, & A. K. Newman,
(c.1825).

Blair, Rev. David (Pseud.).
See Phillips, Sir Richard.

BLOSSOMS OF LEARNING; a new alphabet, in large
type. Dean & Munday, (c.1840).

Boad, Henry.
THE ENGLISH SPELLING BOOK AND EXPOSITOR;
being a new method of teaching children and adult persons
to read, write and understand the English tongue in less
time, and with much greater ease, than has hitherto been
taught. 6th. ed., 1760. 9th. ed., Fuller, Woodfall, etc., 1765.
J. Fuller, 1771. R. Baldwin, 1805. 23rd. ed., 1805.

Bolton, C.
THE IMPERIAL SPELLING BOOK; or, reading made
easy, for the use of schools. Marshall, 1793.

BOWDEN'S INDESTRUCTIBLE BATTLEDORE.
Gainsborough, no date.

THE BRITISH BATTLEDOOR. (c.1810).
With rural view, eight animals.

THE BRITISH BATTLEDORE. Alnwick, Davison, (c.1820).
Printed both sides. Religious text, four wood engravings.

THE BRITISH BATTLEDORE. J. Newbery, 1763.

THE BRITISH BATTLEDORE; or, first lessons. Alnwick, Davison, (c.1830).
Three alphabets, a syllabary, two reading lessons and five Bewick engravings.

Brown, Joseph.
THE FAMILY TESTAMENT AND LEARNER'S ASSISTANT; designed to promote the reading of the Holy Sriptures in families and schools. Listed by Mozley & Sons, 1835.

BROWN'S ROYAL VICTORIA PRIMER; or, child's first book. Whittaker & Co., 1841.

(Budden, Maria E.).
CHIT CHAT, or short tales in short words. J. Harris, 1825, 1831, 1834.

Burden, Mrs.
SHORT TALES IN SHORT WORDS. Dean, (c.1830).

Butter, Henry.
THE ETYMOLOGICAL SPELLING BOOK AND EXPOSITOR. (1830). 21st. ed., 1836. 66th. ed., Simpkin, 1843. 206th. ed., Simpkin, 1856. 1941.

GRADED PRIMER. 10th. ed., Simpkin, 1839.

READING AND SPELLING IN EASY GRADATIONS, upon an entirely new and original plan; by which dissylables are rendered as easy as monosyllables; with numerous entertaining and instructive reading lessons in prose and verse. 1829. 21st. ed., 1839. 35th. ed., 1848.

Carpenter, Thomas.
  AN ENGLISH VOCABULARY. 2nd. ed., Longman,
  1816. Longman, etc., (c.1824).
  THE NEW ORTHOGRAPHICAL ASSISTANT; or,
  English exercise-book. Longman, Hurst, 1807.
  THE NEW ORTHOGRAPHICAL AND
  ORTHOEPICAL ASSISTANT. Hurst, 1803.
  THE SCHOLAR'S SPELLING ASSISTANT.
  C. D. Piguenit, 1796. New Ed., Longman, (c.1824). New
  ed., Longman, 1827. New ed., Longman, etc., 1833, 1834,
  1839. Routledge, (c.1858). Listed by Milner, (c.1860).

CHAMBERS' EDUCATIONAL COURSE:
  ENGLISH: FIRST BOOK OF READING.
          SECOND BOOK OF READING.
          SIMPLE LESSONS IN READING. Orr,
          1836.

THE CHILD'S ALPHABET, emblematically described and
  embellished by twenty-four pictures, brought into easy
  verse, etc. J. E. Evans, (c.1820).

THE CHILD'S BATTLEDORE. Alnwick, Davison, (c.1820)
  Five alphabets and a reading lesson.

THE CHILD'S BATTLEDORE. Alnwick, Davison, (c.1820)
  *Printed both sides. Two alphabets, religious text, eight
  wood engravings.*

THE CHILD'S FIRST BOOK. Derby, Richardson, (c.1835).
  A chapbook.

CHILD'S FIRST BOOK. Banbury, Rusher, (c.1840).
  An alphabet.

THE CHILD'S FIRST BOOK AND SUNDAY-SCHOOL
  PRIMER. T. Hogg, 1835.

THE CHILD'S FIRST BOOK; being an introduction to
  spelling and reading. By the compiler of the Beauties of
  the Children's Friend. Boston, Lincoln & Edmonds, 1816.

THE CHILD'S FIRST BOOK, containing the ABC and a
  set of easy rhymes in one syllable. Webb, Millington,
  (c.1840).

THE CHILD'S FIRST BOOK: containing the alphabet,
  words of two and three letters, and short sentences.
  Glasgow, 1848.

THE CHILD'S FIRST BOOK IMPROVED, with a preface
  addressed to all affectionate mothers and teachers of
  children. 2nd. ed., Vernor & Hood, 1805.

THE CHILD'S FIRST BOOK, or, key to reading, adapted to the capacities of very young children, intended as an introduction to the Mentorian Primer. 10th. ed., Whittaker, (c.1825).

THE CHILD'S FIRST BOOK ; or, reading and spelling made easy. W. S. Johnson, (c.1840).

THE CHILD'S FIRST LESSON BOOK. Bogue. (Lond. Cat.)

THE CHILD'S FIRST STEP TO LEARNING. Wood, (c.1840).

CHILD'S FIRST STEP UP THE LADDER OF LEARNING. Dean & Son, (c.1840).

THE CHILD'S FRIEND; or, reading and spelling made completely easy. Wellington and Iron Bridge, Houlston & Son.

THE CHILD'S INSTRUCTOR; INTENDED AS A FIRST BOOK FOR CHILDREN, WITH SUPERIOR ENGRAVINGS. By a fellow of the Royal Society. 4th. ed., Deal, T. Hayward, 1828.

THE CHILD'S INSTRUCTOR, or picture alphabet. Glasgow, J. Lumsden & Son, (c.1820).
A chapbook; twenty-eight Bewick woodcuts.

THE CHILD'S NEW PLAY-THING; being a spelling-book intended to make learning to read a diversion instead of a task. The second edition; to which is added three dialogues. M. Cooper, 1743. 7th. ed., Ware, 1760. 8th. ed., Ware, Hawes, etc., 1763. Hawes, Clark, etc., 1775. Another edition; THE CHILD'S NEW PLAY-THING, or best amusement. Belfast, D. Wogan, 1819.

THE CHILD'S PICTURE ALPHABET. W. Darton & Son, (c.1835).

THE CHILD'S NEW SPELLING PRIMER; or, first book for children. To which is added the stories of Cinderella, and the Little Red Riding Hood. Dublin, T. Wilkinson, 1799.
Contains alphabets and a syllable exercise.

THE CHILD'S OWN BATTLEDOOR. Darton & Harvey, (c.1798).
Cuts; Squirrel, Peacock, Cat, Parrot.

THE CHILD'S OWN BATTLEDOOR. Darton & Harvey, (c.1810).
Cuts: The Doll, Skittles, Playing at Marbles, Waggon and Horses.

CHILD'S PICTURE READING BOOK, by M.T. Part 2.
Nursery morals chiefly in monosyllables; by the author of
'Always Happy'. J. Harris, 1837.

THE CHILD'S PRIMER. York, Kendrew, 1834.

THE CHILD'S SECOND BOOK, being a sequel to the
first. . . . by J.F., schoolmaster. Penrith, 1806.

Clark, Samuel.
THE CHILD'S TREASURY OF KNOWLEDGE AND
AMUSEMENT; or, Reuben Ramble's picture lessons.
Darton & Clark, (c.1845).
*Four booklets on transportation, birds, other countries,
ABC.*

Clarke, John.
THE RATIONAL SPELLING BOOK, revised by John
Entick. 1791, 1807.

Clarke, Rev. T.
See Galt, John.

CLASSICAL LETTERS, or alphabet of memory; intended
for the instruction and amusement of young gentlemen.
Harris, 1817.
Frontispiece and twenty-three full-page plates in colour.

THE CLASSIFIED SPELLING BOOK. Burns. (Lond.
Cat.)

Cobbet, William.
COBBET'S ENGLISH SPELLING BOOK. Cobbet,
(c.1830).
A SPELLING BOOK, ... with stepping-stones to
English grammar. 1831.
A SPELLING-BOOK, with appropriate lessons in
reading. 2nd. ed., Mills, Jowett & Mills, 1831.

Cobbin, Ingram.
ELEMENTS OF SPELLING AND READING. Ward.
(Lond. Cat.).
GRAMMATICAL AND PRONOUNCING SPELLING
BOOK. Simpkin. (Lond. Cat.).
INSTRUCTIVE READER. F. Westley & A. H. Davies,
1831.
*Cobbin acted as Secretary to the British and Foreign
School Society.*

(Cole, Lady M.F.B.).
THE MOTHER'S PRIMER. By Mrs. Felix Summerley.
Longman, etc., 1844.

Collyer, John.
   READING MADE EASY; or, a preparative for the
   Testament and Bible. 22nd. ed., Nottingham, Burbage
   & Son, 1781. Burbridge & Stretton, 1801.

COMICAL HOTCH-POTCH, or the alphabet turn'd
   posture-master. Carington Bowles, 1782.
   Engraved sheet; posture-master forms shape of letters.
   Descriptive couplet under each.

Commissioners of National Education in Ireland.
   READING LESSON BOOKS:
   FIRST.
   SECOND. Dublin, Falconer, 1855.
   THIRD. Routledge. 1826.
   FOURTH.
   FIFTH.
   SEQUEL TO THE SECOND.
   SUPPLEMENT TO THE FOURTH.
   READING BOOK FOR THE USE OF FEMALE
   SCHOOLS.
   See Committee of Council Schedules of 1847. Listed by
   Groombridge, 1847.

Corner, Julia.
   THE PLAY GRAMMAR, or, the elements of grammar
   explained in easy games. (1848). 11th. ed., enl. and imp.,
   Thos. Dean & Son, (c.1856).

COTTAGE LESSONS, or a second step to learning;
   intended as a sequel to the Cottage Primer. G. Walker,
   1817.

Crossley, J. T.
   COMPREHENSIVE PRIMER, with simple exercises.
   Simpkin, (c.1845).
   COMPREHENSIVE READER IN PROSE AND
   POETRY, with analyses and simultaneous or gallery
   lessons. Simpkin, (c.1845).
   COMPREHENSIVE SPELLING AND READING
   BOOK. Simpkin, (c.1845).
   CROSSLEY'S SEQUEL. Sixty-nine lessons, original or
   compiled, in easy reading. Simpkin, (c.1845).

Cruikshank, George.
   COMIC ALPHABET. Tilt, 1832, 1836.

DAILY LESSON BOOK No. 1, No. 2, No. 3, No. 4. Simpkin, (c.1845).
Used in the schools of the British & Foreign School Society.

DARTON'S SCRIPTURE ALPHABET. Darton & Co., (c.1850).

Davies, T.
THE NEWEST READING MADE COMPLETELY EASY; or, an introduction to reading the Holy Bible. New ed., Gainsborough, 1794. Derby, T. Richardson, 1827. Mozley & Son, 1841.
THE NEWEST READING MADE EASY, or, an introduction to reading the Holy Bible. 53rd. ed., Fourdriniers & Bloxam, (c.1800).

Denham, J.F.
SPELLING AND READING BOOKS. (3). Simpkin. (Lond. Cat.).

DIALOGUES CONSISTING OF WORDS OF ONE SYLLABLE ONLY; intended as a proper book to follow the Imperial Primer. By the author of 'Summer Rambles', etc. Harris, 1816.

Dilworth. T.
A NEW GUIDE TO THE ENGLISH TONGUE. (1740). 13th. ed., H. Kent, 1751. 19th. ed., 1757. R. & H. Cawston, 1784. New ed., with some improvements, Boston, T. & J. Fleet, 1789. For the booksellers, 1795. Stereo ed., A. Wilson, 1812. A. Wilson, for Dean & Munday, (c.1815). In 5 parts, 71st. ed., Neeley & Jones, 1810.

Dixon, H.
THE ENGLISH INSTRUCTOR; or, the art of spelling improved. London, J. Hazard, Bath, J. Leake, 1728. 23rd. ed., 1760. 39th. ed., Rivington, 1801. 68th. ed., 1822.

Duncan, Rev. J.
THE ENGLISH EXPOSITOR; or, a new explanatory spelling book. 5th. ed., Whittaker, (c.1824).

Dyche, Thomas.
A GUIDE TO THE ENGLISH TONGUE, in two parts. (1709). 12th. ed., 1727. 14th. ed., 1729. 16th. ed., 1731. 24th. ed., 1737. Ware, 1740. 43rd. ed., 1760. 48th. ed., C. & R. Ware, 1767. 52nd. ed., corr., Ware, 1769. 56th. ed., Ware, 1771. 1791. T. & M. Robertson, 1796. 102nd. ed., 1800. Corr., enl., imp., Gainsborough, Mozley, 1811.

AN EARLY STAGE ON THE ROAD TO LEARNING; or,
original lessons in words of one and two syllables only,
adapted to the taste and capacity of little children. Harvey
& Darton, 1824.

THE EASTER GIFT; being a useful toy for little Miss and
Master to learn their ABC. J. Catnach, (c.1820).
A chapbook alphabet.

AN EASY INTRODUCTION TO THE ENGLISH
LANGUAGE; or, a pretty entertaining spelling-book for
little masters and misses. Newbery, 1745.
*Vol. 1 of the Circle of the Sciences. Later issued separately
as THE INFANT TUTOR; or, an easy spelling-book for
little masters and misses.*

EASY LESSONS, or leading strings to knowledge. New ed.,
Grant & Griffith, 1848.

AN EASY SPELLING DICTIONARY. Newbery, 1745.
*Later known as SPELLING DICTIONARY OF THE
ENGLISH LANGUAGE ON A NEW PLAN.*

EASY STORIES FOR THE AMUSEMENT AND
INFORMATION OF CHILDREN OF FOUR AND FIVE
YEARS OLD. Hailes, 1831.

Edgeworth, Maria.
EARLY LESSONS. 10 parts in 3 vols. J. Johnson,
1801-03, 1809. 4 vols., 1833-35.

EDINBURGH ALPHABET, and the progress of industry.
Oliver & Boyd, (c.1825).
One of a series of Oliver & Boyd Juvenile Books.

Elliot, Mary (Belson).
EARLY SEEDS TO PRODUCE SPRING FLOWERS.
New ed., Darton, 1824.
PLAIN THINGS FOR LITTLE FOLKS. (1814). Darton,
1823.

England, Rev.
READING BOOK, containing useful and pleasing
lessons. 3rd. ed., Murphy, 1823.

THE ENGLISH BATTLEDORE. Alnwick, Davison,
(c.1820).
*Five alphabets, a syllabary, three reading lessons and list
of consonants. Bewick engravings.*

THE ENGLISH BATTLEDORE. Alnwick, Davison,
(c.1820).
Another version, with text about "our dog Tray".

THE ENGLISH PRIMER, or child's first book; in which are the most easy reading and spelling lessons adapted to promote the first rudiments of learning. Banbury, Rusher, (c.1800).

ENGLISH VOCABULARY, or spelling book, with the meaning attached to each word. Compiled for the use of Ackworth School. Harvey & Darton, (c.1840).

THE ENIGMATICAL ALPHABET, or twenty-five puzzles for a curious boy or girl. Salisbury, C. Fellows, London, J. Wallis, (c.1790).
The answer to each verse-puzzle is a letter of the alphabet.

Entick, John.
THE CHILD'S BEST INSTRUCTOR IN SPELLING AND READING, ETC. London, Edward Dilly, 1757. 6th. ed., 1773.
NEW SPELLING DICTIONARY. Teaching to write and pronounce the English Tongue with ease and propriety. 1764. New ed., 1778. 1781. New, revised ed., Glasgow, Chapman & Lang, for J. Gillies, etc., 1801. A. Wilson, (c.1805). Abridged ed. by T. Ash, 1813. New ed., enlarged by W. Crakelt, 1784, 1787. New ed., to which is prefixed a comprehensive Grammar, 1795, 1800. New ed., edited by Robinson, Dean & Co., (c.1850).

Eves, Charles.
DERIVATIVE SPELLING BOOK. 10th. thou. 1852.
MODERN SPELLING BOOK AND EARLY EDUCATOR. Darton & Clark, 1841.

Fellows, John.
GRADATIONAL SPELLING BOOK. Simpkin. (Lond. Cat.).

Fenn, Lady Eleanor (Frere).
COBWEBS TO CATCH FLIES: or, dialogues in short
sentences . . . . (2 vols.). (1783?) Marshall, 1785, c.1800.
New ed., c. 1815. New ed., Baldwin & Cradock, (2 vols in 1),
1822, 1825, 1829, 1833, 1837. Lockwood & Co., (c.1867).
Also: Selections from ; S.P.C.K., 1844.
Graded Reading Primers. Primary aim was amusement.
Rivalled by Mrs. Barbauld's 'Early Lessons'.
EASY READING, adapted to the capacities of children
from five to seven years old . . . . Being a companion to the
'Little Vocabulary . . . .' By Mrs. Lovechild. 1814.
FABLES IN MONOSYLLABLES, by Mrs. Teachwell.
MORALS TO A SET OF FABLES, by Mrs. Teachwell
(2 in 1 vol.) J. Marshall, (c.1790).
FABLES IN MONOSYLLABLES, by Mrs. Teachwell, to
which are added Fables in Dialogues between a Mother
and Children. J. Marshall, (c.1810).
INFANTINE KNOWLEDGE: a spelling and reading
book on a popular plan. J. Harris, 1837. Grant & Griffith,
(c.1848).
THE INFANT'S FRIEND. Part 1, Spelling Book by
Mrs. Lovechild. Part 2, Reading Lessons. Part 3, Reading
Leasons. E. Newbery, 1799.
THE INFANT'S FRIEND, or easy reading lessons for
young children. Harris 1820. 1824. Grant & Griffith, 1850.
THE LITTLE VOCABULARY, by Mrs. Lovechild. 2nd.
ed., Darton, 1822.
MRS LOVECHILD'S GOLDEN PRESENT, for all good
little boys and girls. York. Kendrew, (c.1820).
A penny chapbook, with picture alphabet and six cuts.
A SPELLING BOOK, designed to render the acquisition
of the rudiments of our native language easy and pleasant
. . . . By Mrs. Teachwell. Marshall, (c.1790).
A SPELLING BOOK, with easy reading lessons . . . .
Harris, 1805.

Fenning, Daniel.
THE NEW AND COMPLETE SPELLING DIC-
TIONARY AND SURE GUIDE TO THE ENGLISH
LANGUAGE, etc. 1767. 2nd. ed., corr. and greatly
enlarged, 1773.
READING MADE PERFECTLY EASY. 1780.
THE UNIVERSAL SPELLING-BOOK, or, a new and
easy guide to the English language. (1755). 4th. ed., 1760.
13th. ed., 1777. S. Jewkes, 1783. New ed., Millar, etc. 1790.
New ed., for the booksellers, 1791. Edited by J. Malham;

Crowder & Colling, 1794. New ed., Lane, 1794. New ed., rev. by R. Jones; Chester, 1801. J. Redwood, 1804. York, 1805. 51st. ed., Paris, J. Malham, 1809. Gainsborough, Mozley, 1812. Liverpool, 1815. Stereo ed., Dublin, 1820. Stereo ed., York, Wilson, 1820. 71st. ed., rev. by Rev. T. Smith, Rivington, 1823. Mozley, 1837. Routledge, (c.1858), 1860. Also IMPROVED UNIVERSAL SPEL-LING BOOK, 27th. ed., Belfast, Simms, 1767.
WOGAN'S IMPROVED SPELLING BOOK. New ed., with addns., Richardson & Son, 1847.

Fenwick, Eliza.
INFANTINE STORIES; in words of one, two and three syllables. (1810). New ed., J. Souter for J. & C. Adlard, (c.1820).

THE FIRST LESSON BOOK. Webb, Millington, (c.1835).

FIRST PHONIC READING BOOK. Compiled by Kay-Shuttleworth. 1843.
A manual for teachers, based on the work done at Batter-sea Training College. Criticised, but greatly helped the acceptance of phonic methods after 1850.

THE FIRST SPELLING BOOK FOR CHILDREN; con-taining a selection of spelling lessons . . . . intended as an introductory assistant to Duncan's English Expositor. Whittaker, 1824.

THE FIRST STEP TO LEARNING; being an easy method of teaching children to read and spell. Derby and London, (c.1835).

Fisher, A.
See Slack, Mrs. Ann.

Fisher, George.
THE INSTRUCTOR; or, young man's best companion. Containing spelling, reading, writing, and arithmetic. (1731?). 27th. ed., 1788. J. Taylor, 1789. 28th. ed., 1798. J. Johnson, 1806.
THE INSTRUCTOR . . . . To which is added, the family's best companion. New ed., London, Osbourne & Griffin; Gainsborough, Mozley, 1797. New ed., corr. by N. Downes, (c.1800).

FISHER'S SPELLING BOOK. No date.

Fletcher, Rev. W.
THE PICTURESQUE PRIMER; or, useful matter made pleasing pastime for leisure hours. Harris, (c.1820). Harris, 1837. Grant & Griffith, (c.1848).

FLORA'S ALPHABET; or the good child's flower garden.
Hodgson, 1822.
*Coloured engraved title, 24 half-page coloured engravings
of flowers.*

Fox, Rev. Francis.
AN INTRODUCTION TO SPELLING AND READING.
7th. ed., 1754. 13th. ed., corr. and imp., Rivington, 1791.
16th. ed., 1802. Rivington, 1808. 20th. ed., 1815.

Free, B. D.
A NEW AND COMPLETE SPELLING DICTIONARY,
and sure guide to the English language, on the plan of the
late Mr. Fenning. 1808.

Fulton, George.
PRONOUNCING SPELLING BOOK, with reading
lessons. 6th. ed., Edinburgh, 1817.

THE FUNNY ALPHABET. Wallis, (c.1821).
*Anecdotes accompany hand-coloured woodcuts of each
letter.*

GAFFER GOODMAN'S PICTURE HORN-BOOKS.
Chapman & Hall, (c.1845).
A progressive series of six folded sheets.

Gall, James.
KEY TO THE BOOK FOR TEACHING CHILDREN TO
READ; with an introductory essay on the fundamental
principles of education. (c.1830). 2nd. ed., Edinburgh, Gall,
1837.

THE GALLOPING GUIDE TO THE ABC, or, the child's
agreeable introduction to a knowledge of the gentlemen of
the alphabet. Banbury, Rusher, (c.1810).
A penny chapbook alphabet.

(Galt, John).
CLARK'S ENGLISH PRIMER, or, child's first book.
Law, (c.1850).
THE NATIONAL READER; consisting of easy lessons
in morals, history, biography, mythology, natural history,
science, and general knowledge, by the Rev. T. Clarke.
Intended as a sequel to THE NATIONAL SPELLING-
BOOK. New ed., imp. and enl. by E. Wickes; Souter, 1833.
Preface dated 1821.

A GENERAL VIEW OF ENGLISH PRONUNCIATION,
to which is added, easy lessons for the use of the English
class. Edinburgh, 1784.

THE GOLDEN ABC. S. Johnson.
A panoramic toy-book.

THE GOLDEN PRIMER; or, an easy and entertaining
guide to the art of reading, for the instruction of all the
good little boys and girls in Great Britain and Ireland.
Printed at Mozley's Lilliputian Book-Manufactory,
Gainsborough, 1788.

THE GOLDEN PRIMER. Darton, 1819.
A coloured battledore.

Goldsmith, Rev. J. (Pseud.).
See Phillips, Sir Richard.

THE GOOD CHILD'S DELIGHT; or Joy to the Eye and
Light to the Mind. A collection of curious engravings and
amusing original stories. Hodgson & Co., (c.1830).
A sixpenny chapbook. Not Dorothy Kilner's book.

THE GOOD CHILD'S REWARD, or, a scriptural alphabet
in verses for children. Chelmsford, Marden, (c.1820).
Two illustrated alphabets, one with verses.

A GOOD LITTLE CHILD'S FIRST ABC. Bishop, (c.1830).

Graham, G. F.
ENGLISH SPELLING, with rules and exercises. Longman, 1847.

GRANDMAMMA EASY'S ALDERMAN'S FEAST: a
new alphabet. Dean & Co., (c.1840).
*Grandmamma Easy's new pictorial toy books. Text in
verse; eight pages, eight woodcuts.*

GRANDMAMMA EASY'S NEW STORY ABOUT
LITTLE JACK HORNER. Dean & Co., (c.1840).
Large type, coloured engravings.

GRANDMAMMA EASY'S PRETTY POETICAL SPELLING BOOK, ABOUT TREES, FRUIT AND FLOWERS. Dean & Co., (c.1840).
Eight pages, printed on one side only. 27 woodcuts.

GREEN'S FIRST TALES FOR LITTLE CHILDREN. Darton & Clark, (c.1840).
With seven coloured plates.

GREEN'S NURSERY LEADING STRINGS. THE ALPHABET. Dean & Co., (c.1840).
Eight leaves, woodcut title, two cuts on each page.

GREEN'S UNIVERSAL PRIMER, or Child's First Book. Darton & Clark, (c.1840).

Greig, John.
THE EXPEDITIOUS SELF-INSTRUCTOR; containing the elements of reading, grammar, writing, (illustrated with copies,) arithmetic, (with tables,) geography and the globes, history and chronology, (with a table,) with a great variety of forms useful in business. The whole explained in a most familiar manner, in order to enable those to instruct themselves, who have not the opportunity of masters. New ed., Simpkin & Marshall, (c.1824).

Guy, Joseph.
THE NEW BRITISH EXPOSITOR. Cradock & Co., 1826.
THE NEW BRITISH READER. Cradock, 1835.
GUY'S NEW BRITISH SPELLING BOOK ; or, an easy introduction to spelling and reading, in seven parts. 2nd. ed., Cradock & Joy, 1810. 35th. ed., Baldwin & Cradock, 1832. 37th. ed., 1834. 61st. ed., rev., Cradock & Co., 1842. Listed by Milner, (c.1860).
GUY'S NEW EXERCISES IN ORTHOGRAPHY. Baldwin, Cradock & Joy, 1818.
ROYAL VICTORIA SPELLING BOOK. Cradock. (Lond. Cat.).

Harland, W.
  THE CHILD'S ASSISTANT: or, a most easy introduction to reading the English language. Scarborough, Ainsworth, 1828.

HARLEQUIN'S ABC. J. Innes, (c.1840). W. S. Johnson, (c.1850).
  Drawings of one or two people contorting themselves into letters.

HARRISON'S JUVENILE INSRUCTOR, or first book for children. Devizes, J. Harrison, (c.1830).

HARRY'S LADDER TO LEARNING: Harry's Hornbook; Harry's Picture Book; Harry's Nursery Songs; Harry's Simple Stories. (4 in 1 vol.) Bogue, 1849.
  With about 180 coloured illustrations. Later listed as:

HARRY'S LADDER TO LEARNING. Picture books for children. Harry's Own Book, Harry's Picture Book, Harry's Country Walks, Harry's Nursery Songs, Harry's Simple Stories, Harry's Nursery Tales. Separately, or in one volume. W. Kent & Co. (late D. Bogue) 1854.

Hastie, T.
  THE ONLY METHOD TO MAKE READING EASY, or, child's best instructor. Newcastle, Angus, (c.1780). 73rd. ed., Newcastle, Charnley, 1839.
  Twenty-four cuts by Bewick of animals and birds illustrate the alphabet.

Hewlett, John.
  AN INTRODUCTION TO READING AND SPELLING. 4th. ed., 1798. Rev., enl., 1816.

THE HISTORICAL ALPHABET. Harris, 1812.
  With twenty-six full-page coloured engravings of historical scenes.

THE HISTORY OF A APPLE PIE. S. C. Bysh, (c.1830).

THE HISTORY OF AN APPLE PIE. J. L. Marks, (c.1835).
  Poem 'Evening Hymn' on lower cover.

THE HISTORY OF THE APPLE PIE, WRITTEN BY Z. Harris, 1808.

THE HISTORY OF LITTLE MARY AND HER DOLL JANE, a new pleasing and complete nursery alphabet. J. Bailey, (c.1810).

Hornsey, John.
 THE BOOK OF MONOSYLLABLES; or, an introduction
 to the Child's Monitor, adapted to the capacities of very
 young children. In two parts. York, 1807. Listed by Longmans, 1838. Also known as FIRST GUIDE TO
 READING.
 THE CHILD'S MONITOR; or, parental instruction. In
 five parts, containing great variety of progressive lessons,
 adapted to the comprehension of children: calculated to
 instruct them in reading, in the use of stops, in spelling,
 and in dividing words into proper syllables; etc. 2nd. ed.,
 York, for Longman, etc., 1809. New ed., Longman, etc.,
 (c.1824).
 THE PRONOUNCING EXPOSITOR; or, a new spelling
 book. In three parts. 7th. ed., Longman, etc., (c.1824).

Hort, William Jillard.
 HORT'S EASY COURSE OF DOMESTIC
 EDUCATION:
  Book 2, ENGLISH SPELLING BOOK. Longman, 1822
  Book 3, INTRODUCTORY READING BOOK.
  Longman, 1822.

THE HOUSE THAT JACK BUILT. G. Mansell, (c.1840).
 With twelve wood engravings and two alphabets.

HOWE'S PRIMER, or, the child's first book. Derby,
 William Bemrose & Co., (c.1830).

(Hughes, Mary).
 AUNT MARY'S NEW YEAR'S GIFT. For little boys and
 girls who are learning to read. Darton, (c.1850).
 AUNT MARY'S STORIES FOR CHILDREN, chiefly
 confined to words of two syllables. W. Darton & Son,
 (c.1835).

HUMPTY DUMPTY'S GOLDEN ABC. A. Park, (c.1840).

THE ILLUSTRATED ABC, or the child's first step to learning. Sudbury, H. M. Ives, (c.1850).

THE ILLUSTRATED LONDON SPELLING BOOK. Illustrated London News, 1849. 57th. thou. 1850.

THE IMPERIAL ALPHABET; or, good child's delight. Hodgson & Co., 1823.

THE IMPERIAL BATTLEDOOR. (c.1800).

THE IMPERIAL BATTLEDORE. Newbery, 1763.

THE INDESTRUCTIBLE ALPHABET. Cundall & Addey, (c.1850).

THE INDESTRUCTABLE READING BOOK. Addey, (c.1850).

THE INDESTRUCTABLE SPELLING BOOK. Cundall & Addey, (c.1850).
These three books are printed on linen.

INFANTINE KNOWLEDGE, a Spelling Book, edited by Thomas Smith. 2nd. ed., J. Harris, (c.1830).

THE INFANT'S ALPHABET. Dean & Munday, 1823.
Rhyming couplets.

THE INFANT'S ALPHABET. Harvey & Darton, (c.1840).
On a sheet, 6d. Dissected, (jig-saw) 3/6d.

THE INFANT'S BATTLEDORE, a present for a good child. Castle Cary, S. Moore, (c.1825).

THE INFANT'S BATTLEDORE, for a good child. Castle Cary, S. Moore, (c.1825).

THE INFANT'S BATTLEDORE, for a good child at school. Castle Cary, S. Moore, (c.1825).

THE INFANT'S LIBRARY:
Book 1; ILLUSTRATED ALPHABET. J. Marshall, (c.1785). E. Marshall, (c.1802). J. Marshall, 1821.
Book 2; SYLLABLES AND SHORT WORDS.
Altogether 16 books.

THE INFANT'S PATH STREWED WITH FLOWERS. Marshall, 1822.

THE INFANT'S PATH, STREWN WITH FLOWERS. Marshall, 1820.

THE INFANT'S PRIMER. E. Marshall, (c.1830).

THE INFANT'S TOY BOOK. Dean, (c.1825).
With sixteen half-page hand-coloured cuts.

THE INFANT'S TOY BOOK OF PRETTY TALES. A. K. Newman & Co., (c.1830).

THE INFANT'S TUTOR. J. Bysh, (c.1805).
A picture-reading book.

Innes, Henry.
THE BRITISH CHILD'S SPELLING BOOK. 3rd. ed., 1835.
BRITISH YOUTH'S READER. Limbird, 1835.
INNES'S BRITISH MINERVA PRIMER, or, London first book for children. (c.1830).

INSTRUCTION AND AMUSEMENT UNITED; or, reading made easy, Huddersfield, J. Brook, (c.1790).

INTRODUCTION TO SPELLING. Morpeth, Markham, 1824.

JACK DANDY'S DELIGHT. York, Kendrew, (c.1830).
A chapbook; alphabet, rhymes, precepts and descriptions of animals.

James, S.
DILWORTH IMPROVED, or a New Guide to the English Tongue. Whittingham, 1810.

Jameson, Anna Brownwell (Murphy).
A FIRST, OR MOTHER'S DICTIONARY FOR CHILDREN; containing upwards of three thousand eight hundren words which occur most frequently in books and conversation . . . . The whole adapted to the capacities of younger children. Darton, (c.1815). 2nd. ed., 1824. 4th. ed., (c.1840).

JENNY WREN ALPHABET. Otley, Walker & Son, (c.1835).
With three nursery rhymes.

Johnson, C. W.
ENGLISH RURAL SPELLING BOOK. 1846.
Listed in Committee of Council schedules, 1847.

Jones, E.
THE OXFORD SPELLING-BOOK; or, the complete English tutor. Law, 1770.

THE JUVENILE KEEPSAKE. Glasgow, 1850.

JUVENILE MANUAL OF READING. Longman. (Lond. Cat.).

JUVENILE STORIES AND DIALOGUES, composed chiefly in words of two syllables .... Vernon & Hood, 1799. Vernon, Hood & E. Newbery, 1801.

Kay, R.
   THE NEW PRECEPTOR; or, young lady's and gentlemen's true instructor in the rudiments of the English tongue. Newcastle, Angus, 1801.
   Probably the first attempt at a phonic method in this country.

Keble, T. H.
   KEBLE'S NEW PRIMER; or, reading made easy. Margate, Keble, (c.1845).
   KEBLE'S SECOND BRITISH SPELLING BOOK. London & Margate, Keble, (c.1850).

Keys, Adam.
   THE EXCITEMENT; or, a book to induce boys to read .. .. Edinburgh, Waugh & Innes, 1830.

A KEY TO KNOWLEDGE, or things in common use, simply and shortly explained in a series of dialogues, written by a mother. 3rd. ed., rev. by the author, 1820.

Kilner, Dorothy.
   THE GOOD CHILD'S DELIGHT; or, the road to knowledge, in short entertaining lessons of one and two syllables. Marshall, (c.1785). New ed., Baldwin, Cradock and Joy, and N. Hailes, 1819.
   Very popular and much copied. Not to be confused with
   THE GOOD CHILD'S DELIGHT; *or , joy to the eye and light to the mind; Hodgson, Juvenile Press, (c.1830), which was a sixpenny chapbook.*
   LITTLE STORIES FOR LITTLE FOLKS IN EASY LESSONS OF ONE, TWO AND THREE SYLLABLES. J. Marshall, (c.1790), 1806.

KING ARTHUR'S ALPHABET. Low & Co., (c.1850).

THE LADY-BIRD'S LOTTERY, or the Fly's alphabet, by Queen Mab. Macdonald & Son, for Longman, etc., 1813.

Lamont, Mrs.
TEACHER'S TREASURE. A reading-book for slow learners. On a novel plan. Harvey & Darton, (c.1840).

Lancaster, Joseph.
A SPELLING BOOK. Harvey, (c.1840).

LEIGHTON'S NEW BATTLEDORE. Nottingham, (c.1830).
Spelling lists, six woodcuts, Lord's Prayer, two reading lessons and two poems.

Leitch, Neil.
THE JUVENILE READER; consisting of religious, moral, and intellectual instruction; exercises in spelling, explanation, and derivation. Glasgow, John Burnet, William Collins, 1839. 75th. thou., 1852.
Listed in the Committee of Council schedules of 1847.
THE MONITORIAL CLASS BOOKS; being an easy introduction to English reading, etc. (In 3 parts.) Glasgow, Collins etc., 1825. Part 1, 25th, ed., 1848. Part 2, 35th. ed., 1852. Part 3, 21st. ed., 1852.
PRACTICAL AND ECONOMICAL READERS. Collins, 1836.
THE YOUNG SCHOLAR'S SPELLING BOOK. (c.1830). Glasgow, 10th. thou. 1852.

Lenoir, P. V.
THE LOGOGRAPHIC EMBLEMATICAL ENGLISH SPELLING BOOK, or a method of teaching children to read. Boosey, 1800. Baldwin, (c.1840).

LESSONS IN READING FOR CHILDREN IN FAMILIES AND SCHOOLS. R.T.S., 1842.
With questions on each passage.

LESSONS ON COMMON THINGS FOR LITTLE CHILDREN. Darton, (c.1825).
150 common objects illustrated by 12 coloured plates.

THE LIFE AND DEATH OF A, APPLE PIE. A. K. Newman, 1823.

THE LIFE AND DEATH OF AN APPLE-PIE. Carvalho, (c.1825).

THE LIFE AND DEATH OF JENNY WREN. York, Kendrew.

THE LIFE AND HISTORY OF A, APPLE-PIE, who was cut to pieces and eaten by twenty-six young ladies and gentlemen, with whom all little people ought to be acquainted. Dean & Munday, (c.1822), (c.1830).

Limming, W.
GOOD AND BAD, or which to follow and what to avoid. Related chiefly in monosyllables and adapted to the infant capacity. Dean & Munday, (c.1840).
With twelve coloured engravings.

THE LITTLE CHILD'S TUTOR, or first book for children, in words not exceeding two syllables. Derby, H. Mozley & Sons, 1845.

THE LITTLE CHRISTIAN'S SUNDAY ALPHABET. By a Lady. Wertheim & Macintosh, 2nd. ed., 1850.

LITTLE FRANK AND OTHER TALES. In words of one syllable. Harvey & Darton, (c.1840).

LITTLE JACK'S PRIMER. Marsh, (c.1840).

LITTLE JANE. Bishop & Co., 1840.

LITTLE LESSONS FOR LITTLE FOLK. In words of one or two syllables. J. Marshall, 1819.
32 pages. Not to be confused with 'LITTLE LESSONS FOR LITTLE FOLKS' by Mary Elliot.

THE LITTLE LOTTERY BOOK FOR CHILDREN: containing a new method of playing them into a knowledge of the letters, figures, etc. J. Newbery, 1756.

LITTLE MARY'S BOOKS FOR CHILDREN. Primer, Spelling-book, Reading-book, History of England, Scripture Lessons, First Book of Poetry, Second Book of Poetry, Babes in the Wood, Picture Riddles, Little Mary and Her Doll, Natural History. LITTLE MARY'S LESSON BOOK, containing Primer, Spelling and Reading in 1 vol. LITTLE MARY'S TREASURY; 8 of Little Mary's Books in 1 vol. Listed by W. Kent & Co. (late D. Bogue), 1854. LITTLE MARY'S PRIMER, Bogue, 1847.

THE LITTLE PRIMER. S. Marks, and sons of J. L. Marks, (c.1830).
A chapbook.

LITTLE SPELLING BOOK, or child's best instructor; a pleasing introduction to spelling and reading. Bath, Steart & Pyrry, (c.1780).

LITTLE STORIES OF ONE AND TWO SYLLABLES, for little children. Masters, 1849.
With nine full-page coloured cuts.

LITTLE SUSAN: a tale in easy words, for children under six years of age. By Aunt Sophy. Hooper, 1842.

THE LITTLE TEACHER, FOR READING AND SPELLING WELL. By a parent. Darton & Harvey, 1798.

THE LITTLE TEACHER, or child's first spelling book. Darton, Harvey & Darton, 1814.

Lloyd, W. F.
HELP FOR INFANTS IN SPELLING, READING AND THINKING. Hamilton. (Lond. Cat.).

LONDON BATTLEDORE. No imprint. (c.1840).

THE LONDON NEW BATTLEDORE. Penryn, White-horn, (c.1830).

Lovechild, Mrs.
See Fenn.

Lowe, S.
THE CRITICAL SPELLING BOOK. 1775. 2nd. ed., 1779.

Maccrea, John.
PRONOUNCING SPELLING BOOK. Simms, etc., (c.1840).

MAJA'S ALPHABET. Illustrated with twenty-six pictures. Cundall & Addey and David Bogue, (c.1850).

MAMA'S LESSONS FOR HER LITTLE BOYS AND GIRLS. Harris, 1835. 9th. ed., Grant & Griffith, 1846.
With sixteen full-page coloured engravings.

Books which were used for the Teaching of Reading

Manson, David
DIRECTIONS TO PLAY THE LITERARY CARDS,
invented for the improvement of children in learning and
morals, from their beginning to learn the letters, till they
become proficient in spelling, reading, parsing, and arithmetic. (Together with a set of 119 cards.) Printed for the
author, 1764.
A NEW SPELLING BOOK; containing above six
thousand familiar words, arranged in tables according to
the tones of the vowels, with a variety of reading lessons.
(c.1760). Dublin, T. Tegg, 1839.
MANSON'S SPELLING BOOK REVISED, etc., Belfast,
1826.

Marcet, Jane (Haldimand).
THE MOTHER'S FIRST BOOK; containing reading
made easy, and the spelling book, in two parts. Longman,
etc., 1845.

Markham, William.
AN INTRODUCTION TO SPELLING AND READING
ENGLISH. (c.1720). 5th. ed., 1738. 34th. ed., Gains-
borough, Mozley, 1790. 35th. ed., London, Osborne &
Griffin; Gainsborough, Mozley, 1792. Pratt, 1814.
Morpeth, Blair, 1824. Routledge, (c.1858).

MARK'S UNIVERSAL PRIMER AND PREPARATORY
SPELLING BOOK. Mark.

Marks, Edward N.
THE EAR AND THE EYE, OR A NEW WAY TO TRY.
Nelson, (c.1850).
*Subtitled: 'A picture printer in rhyme, in which no word
exceeds three letters.' Has ornamental alphabet.*

Marshall, C.
AN INTRODUCTION TO THE ENGLISH TONGUE;
designed for a spelling book, suited to the tender
capacities of children, etc. Bew, (c.1780).

MARTIN'S NURSERY BATTLEDOOR. G. Martin,
(c.1810).

MARTIN'S PICTURE BATTLEDORE FOR THE
NURSERY. G. Martin, (c.1810).

MARY AND HER CAT, in words not exceeding two
syllables. Darton, 1821.

Masson, Arthur.
  AN ENGLISH SPELLING BOOK, for the use of schools.
  2nd. ed., Edinburgh, Hamilton, Balfour & Neill, 1757.
  In three parts. 14th. ed., corr. and impr., to which is now
  added a collection of fables. Perth, Morison & Son, 1794.

Maunder, Samuel.
  UNIVERSAL CLASS BOOK. Longman, 1844. 1847.

Mavor, William Fordyce.
  THE ENGLISH SPELLING BOOK. Phillips, 1801. 32nd.
  ed., rev., Phillips, 1806. 136th. ed., 1812. 1814. 277th. ed.,
  Longman, 1822. 296th ed., Longman, 1824. 322nd. ed.,
  1826. 352nd. ed., Longman, 1829. Alnwick, Davison, 1830.
  375th. ed., Longman, 1831. 443rd. ed., rev., Longman,
  1838. Bristol, 1840. Derby and London, Mozley, 1855.
  New ed., Wood, n.d. Routledge, (c.1858). William Tegg,
  (c.1865). Illustrated by Kate Greenaway, Routledge, 1885.
  Routledge, 1900. Edited by P. A. Nutall; Warne & Co.,
  (c.1902). Warne & Co., (c.1912).
  *Probably the most successful spelling book; certainly the
  most famous. Spielmann and Layard thought it 'One of
  the most inspiring school-books ever published.' Its
  success encouraged the persistence of the spelling method
  of teaching reading.*
  THE ENGLISH SPELLING BOOK, to which is added a
  Concise Treatise on Arithmetic by John Spanton. Derby,
  Richardson, (c.1840).
  MAVOR'S EASY SPELLING BOOK. Bishop & Co.,
  (c.1830).
  A chapbook.
  MAVOR'S FIRST BOOK FOR CHILDREN, intended as
  an introduction to a correct knowledge of the English
  language. New ed., for the booksellers, (c.1850).
  A chapbook; 16 pages.
  MAVOR'S FIRST SPELLING BOOK, etc. Dr. Mavor's
  School, Hurley, Berks., (c.1840).
  MAVOR'S NEW LONDON SPELLING BOOK. G.
  Ingram, (c.1840).
  THE NEW SPEAKER, OR ENGLISH CLASS-BOOK.
  2nd. ed., 1803. 4th. ed., 1811.

Mayhew, Henry.
  THE PRINCE OF WALES' PRIMER. New ed., Grant &
  Griffith, 1847.

M'Culloch, Rev. John Murray.
  A COURSE OF ELEMENTARY READING IN
  SCIENCE AND LITERATURE.Edinburgh, 1827.
  5th. ed.,impr., Edinburgh, Oliver & Boyd, 1834.
  Listed in the Committee of Council schedules of 1847.
  SERIES OF READING LESSONS:
    FIRST READING BOOK. Oliver & Boyd. 16th. ed.
    1852.
    SECOND READING BOOK. Oliver & Boyd.
    A THIRD READING-BOOK FOR THE USE OF
    SCHOOLS, containing simple pieces in prose and verse,
    with exercises on the more difficult words and sounds.
    1837. 19th. ed., Oliver & Boyd, 1853.
    SERIES OF LESSONS IN PROSE AND VERSE.
  *This series is listed in the Committee of Council schedules
  of 1847.*

Meeke, Mrs.
  MAMA'S GIFT; or, pleasing lessons, adapted for children
  of an early age. Dean & Munday, (c.1820).

THE MODERN PICTURE ALPHABET OF CURIO-
  SITIES. March, (c.1840).
  A picture alphabet and first reader.

Moore, J. S.
  A NEW SPELLING BOOK OF THE ENGLISH
  LANGUAGE, etc. Smith, etc., 1838.

Mortimore, Favell Lee (Bevan).
  READING DISENTANGLED; a series of elementary
  reading lessons on sheets. 2nd series, Roake & Narty,
  (c.1836). 14th. ed., 1855. 1873.
  Listed in the Committee of Council schedules of 1847.
  READING WITHOUT TEARS; or, a pleasant mode of
  learning to read. (1850). Hatchard, 1857. Harchard, 1861.
  Hatchard, 1870-75. 76th. thou., 1888. Longman, Green,
  1904. Longman, 1933.
  *The first fully-fledged and successful phonic method in
  this country.*

MOTHER MUGGINS AND HER DOG TRAP'S ABC.
  Ryle & Co., (c.1845).

MOZLEY'S FIRST BOOK FOR CHILDREN, or reading
  made perfectly easy. 69th. ed., Derby, Mozley, 1824.

Murray, Lindley.
ENGLISH READER. York, 1799. 14th. ed., 1817.
AN ENGLISH SPELLING BOOK; with reading lessons
adapted to the capacities of children; in three parts . . . .
York, 1804. 10th. ed., 1810. 14th. ed., 1812. Longman,
(c.1824).
FIRST BOOK, FOR CHILDREN. Longman, etc.,
(c.1824). 17th. ed., York, 1825.

Murray, T. B.
ALPHABET OF EMBLEMS, IN VERSE. Rivington,
(c.1840).

THE MURRAY ALPHABET; or pleasing pictures. Blake,
(c.1815).
With twelve engravings.

MY FIRST LESSON BOOK TO TEACH ME SPELLING
AND READING. Keble, (c.1850).
*Alphabet in capitals, cyllable exercises, monosyllabic
words for handwriting.*

Mylne, William.
Spelling (in two parts). Blackwood. (Lond.Cat.).

MY NEW BATTLEDORE. Kettering, Joseph Toller,
(c.1825).

MY OWN ALPHABET OF HISTORY. Cowan & Standring,
(c.1840).
The Toyman's Picture Books series. Rhyming text.

A NEW AND ENTERTAINING ALPHABET FOR
YOUNG CHILDREN, where some instruction may be
gained, and much amusement. Darton, 1813.

A NEW AND PLEASING INTRODUCTION TO
READING: designed to conduct the youthful mind into a
progressive acquaintance with the knowledge of letters,
the sound of syllables, and the use of words. Bocking, J. F.
Shearcroft, 1837.

NEW BATTLEDORE. Alnwick, W. Davison, (c.1830).

NEW BATTLEDORE. Birmingham, T. Bloomer, (c.1830).
Outer: fifteen woodcuts with captions. Inner: four verses with woodcuts; numerals, one to nullo.

NEW BATTLEDORE. Birmingham, T. Bloomer, (c.1830).
Three alphabets, two reading lessons, two woodcuts, three verses.

Newbery, John.
THE LADDER TO LEARNING. Step the first; being a collection of select fables, consisting of words of only one syllable. Step the second; being a collection of select fables, with original morals, upon a new plan, consisting of words not exceeding two syllables. Step the third; being a collection of select fables; intended as an easy introduction to the art of reading. E. Newbery, 1789.
THE LADDER TO LEARNING. A select collection of fables, consisting of words of one, two, and three syllables; with original morals on a new plan. Ornamented with a great variety of engravings on wood. J. Harris, 1802.
See also Mrs. Trimmer.
A LITTLE PRETTY POCKET-BOOK. 1744. 1747. 1752. 1756. 1760. 1763. 1767. 1770. 1783.
Perhaps the most famous of early children's books.

THE NEW ENGLISH SPELLING BOOK; with a critical analysis of the language, and a classification of its elements. 1846.

THE NEW EXPOSITOR, containing tables of words from two to seven syllables. 7th. ed., Liverpool, 1806.

THE NEW EXPOSITOR; containing tables of words from one to seven syllables inclusive, accented and divided according to the most improved method of pronunciation .... To which is added, tables of synonymous words .... Originally compiled by Messrs. Ashton and Cleg. Rev., corr. and impr. by J. Knowles, 44th. ed., Derby, Mozley, (c.1835).

A NEW INVENTED HORN BOOK. (c.1820).
Alphabet, upper and lower case; vowels; syllable exercise; Lord's Prayer; A Apple, B Ball, etc.

THE NEW LONDON ALPHABET. W. S. Johnson, (c.1850).

THE NEW LONDON ALPHABET, IN RHYME, with twenty-eight pictures of the principal places in that far-famed city. Darton, (c.1850).

THE NEW LONDON READING, made completely easy. Evans, (18th. c.).

THE NEW LONDON READING MADE EASY, or, the child's own book, to which is added select pieces of poetry and the church catechism. New ed., (c.1820).

A NEW LOTTERY BOOK ON A PLAN ENTIRELY NEW. Edinburgh, Caw & Elder, 1819.

THE NEW PARLOUR SPELLING GAME, or reading made easy. (c.1850).

NEW PENNY BATTLEDORE. Otley, Walker, (c.1830).

A NEW PLAY BOOK FOR CHILDREN, or an easy and natural introduction to the art of reading. In which is introduced a great variety of prudential and proverbial maxims, with several little moral tales and fables in prose and verse in order to render their little lessons a diversion rather than a task. Thos. Harris, 1749.

THE NEW PRIMER, in words of one syllable. Derby, Mozley.

THE NEW READING MADE EASY, consisting of a variety of useful lessons. Alnwick, Davison, (c.1820).

THE NEW RHYMING ALPHABET, or the invitation of A to all the letters. Dean & Munday, (c.1820).

THE NEW ROYAL BATTLEDORE. Kettering, Joseph Toller, (c.1825).

A NEW SEQUEL TO MRS. BARBAULD'S LESSONS, adapted to children from four to seven years old. Nottingham, Sutton, 1796. 2nd. ed., enl. G. Sael, 1796.

THE NEW UNIVERSAL PRIMER. Derby, (c.1820).

THE NOTTINGHAM NEW READING MADE EASY: or, first book for children; containing the most plain and easy lessons in reading and spelling. Nottingham, C.N. Wright, 1820.

No. 7 NEW BATTLEDORE. Derby, Mozley, (c.1840).

NURSERY LEADING STRINGS. The little reader, in large type. Darton & Co., (c.1840).
With eight large woodcuts.

NURSERY READING IN WORDS NOT EXCEEDING FOUR LETTERS. E.Wallis, (c.1835).

THE OFFICER'S DAUGHTERS, or Emily and Kitty; in
  words of three syllables. Miller, (c.1820).

OPEN AND SEE; or, first reading lessons. Harvey &
  Darton, (c.1840).

THE ORIGINAL READING MADE EASY IMPROVED.
  Beilby & Knotts, (c.1825).

Osbourne, Charles.
  A PICTORIAL ALPHABET. Osbourne & Ackermann,
  1840.
  *Letters of alphabet engraved on separate cards, booklet of
  explanation.*

Paley, William.
  THE YOUNG CHRISTIAN INSTRUCTED IN
  READING. 1790. Later known as:
  READING MADE COMPLETELY EASY, or, a neces-
  sary introduction to reading the Bible . . . . C. D. Piguenit,
  1791. March & Co., 1792. Crosby, 1806. Johnson, (c.1855).

PAPA'S GIFT FOR A GOOD CHILD. Johnson, (c.1840).
  A pictorial alphabet.

THE PARENT'S BEST GIFT; containing the church catechism. Derby, Richardson & Co., (c.1825). Another
  edition: York, Kendrew, c.1820.
  With alphabets on inner covers.

THE PARLOUR TEACHER. Darton & Harvey, 1804.
  Reading lessons in prose and verse.

THE PATENT INDESTRUCTABLE PRIMER. Cundall &
  Bogue, (c.1850).
  Printed on linen.

PATHS OF LEARNING STREWN WITH FLOWERS, or,
  English grammar illustrated. Harris & Son, 1820.

Pelham, Margaret.
  THE LONDON PRIMER; or, a first book for children at a
  very early age. 40th. ed., Phillips, etc., 1809.

PETER PARLEY'S PRIMER, AND LADDER TO
  LEARNING, or alphabet in verse. Lacey, (c.1835).
  A coloured woodcut for each letter.

PETER PIPER'S PRACTICAL PRINCIPLES OF PLAIN
AND PERFECT PRONUNCIATION. J. Harris & Son,
1813. Harris, 1819. Harris, 1820. 1822.
Harris's Cabinet of Amusement and Instruction, No. 8.
The best-known verse is 'Peter Piper pick'd a Peck of
Pepper!'

PETER PRATTLE'S NAVAL ABC. S. Lingham, (c.1840).

(Phillips, Sir Richard).
THE CLASS BOOK; or, three hundred and sixty-five
reading lessons adapted to the use of schools. By Rev.
David Blair. Phillips, 1806. 3rd. ed., 1807. 10th. ed.,
Phillips, 1811. 12th. ed., Longman, 1814. New ed.,
(c.1819). Longman, 1820. New ed., Longman, 1823. New
ed., Longman, 1830.
THE FIRST STEP TO KNOWLEDGE; being an easy
introduction to the various English spelling books. By
Rev. J. Goldsmith. W. & T. Darton, 1810. W. Darton,
1813. New ed., Darton, (c.1850).
READING EXERCISES FOR SCHOOLS, on a new and
very popular plan, being a sequel to Mavor's Spelling, and
an introduction to the Class Book, similar in arrangement
to Brown's testament. By Rev. David Blair. (c.1819). 21st
ed., Longman, (c.1824).

THE PHONETIC SPELLING BOOK, exhibiting all the
monosyllables of the English language, under a four-fold
arrangement, etc. Bath, 1843.

THE PHONOGRAPHIC AND PHONOTYPIC ALPHA-
BETS. Bath, Pitman; London, Bagster & Sons, 1845.

Pickburn, John.
THE MORAL INSTRUCTOR; or, a collection of sentences from the best authors, disposed in easy lessons for
children. 1759. 7th. ed., Boston, J. Hallaby, 1805. 7th. ed.,
Louth, J. & J. Jackson, 1828.

THE PICTURE ALPHABET. Derby, Richardson, (c.1830).
A chapbook.

THE PICTURE ALPHABET FOR THE ENTERTAIN-
MENT AND INSTRUCTION OF CHILDREN IN THE
NURSERY. Houlston, n.d.
A twopenny chapbook.

PICTORIAL PANORAMIC ALPHABET FOR VERY
LITTLE FOLKS. Dean & Son.
Amusing panoramas of animals, No. 12.

THE PICTURE ALPHABET. Bishop & Co., (c.1830).
A chapbook.

THE PICTURE ALPHABET. Glasgow, 1848.

THE PICTURE ALPHABET, IN PROSE AND VERSE.
R. T. S., 1834.
*A religious text and short verse for each letter of the
alphabet.*

THE PICTURE SHOP FOR GOOD CHILDREN. Darton,
(c.1820).
Thirty-two engravings, alphabets at beginning and end.

PICTURES AND POETRY FOR CHILDREN. Darton,
1837.
Two alphabets, poems, cuts of animals and birds.

THE PICTURESQUE PRIMER, or, first steps up the
ladder of learning. J. Harris, 1834.

PIGEON PIE ALPHABET. Otley, W. Walker & Son,
(c.1835).

Pinnock, William.
THE EXPLANATORY ENGLISH SPELLING BOOK,
etc. Whittaker, Treacher, 1833.
INTRODUCTION TO THE EXPLANATORY
SPELLING BOOK. Alton, 1810. 8th. ed., Whittaker,
(c.1824).
THE MENTORIAN PRIMER; or, Pinnock's second book
for children at an early age. Whittaker, (c.1824).
PINNOCK'S EXPLANATORY ENGLISH READER
AND UNIVERSAL CLASSBOOK. 7th. ed., corr. and
enl., Whittaker, etc., 1832.
PINNOCK'S JUVENILE READER; being a sequel to
the Mentorian Primer. 9th. ed., imp., Whittaker, (c.1824).
THE UNIVERSAL EXPLANATORY ENGLISH
READER. Winchester, Pinnock, 1813. 5th. ed., enl., 1821.
6th. ed. listed Whittaker, (c.1824).
THE UNIVERSAL EXPLANATORY SPELLING
BOOK, with key and exercises. Alton, Pinnock, 1810.
10th. ed., listed Whittaker, 1824.

Platts, Rev. John W.
THE FEMALE MENTOR, or ladies' class book. Derby,
Mozley, (c.1835).
THE NEW JUVENILE READER, for the use of
schools and private teachers; being a sequel to all spelling
books. Derby, Mozley, (c.1824). 4th. ed., listed 1835.

THE PLEASING INSTRUCTOR. Knight & Bagster for
J. Davis, 1825.
Sixteen pages; not Mrs. Slack's Pleasing Instructor.

POEMS, PICTURES, AND ALPHABET OF VERSES.
Chelmsford, Marsden, (c.1820).
A chapbook.

THE POSTURE MASTER'S GRAND MUSEUM, or a
comical alphabet. Newry, J. Stephenson, 1821.

A PRESENT FROM WINDSOR FOR GOOD BOYS AND
GIRLS, written in words of one syllable only. New ed.,
A. Chapman, 1825.

PRIMER, or, child's best guide, containing the most
familiar words of one syllable. Originally compiled by
D. Manson, Belfast. Dublin, 1845.
Uses old blocks.

THE PRIMMER, corrected and improved. Greenock,
W. McAlpine, 1781.
*The spelling of the title may indicate that the word was
pronounced differently in the eighteenth century.*

PRINCE ARTHUR'S ALPHABET; or, A was an archer.
Dean, (c.1850).
A 'moveable'.

A PROGRESSIVE SPELLING BOOK, commencing with
words of two letters, and proceeding . . . . to those of seven
syllables. 2nd. ed., Stourport, 1810.

PRONUNCIATION TAUGHT AS AN AMUSEMENT, by
means of cuts by an indulgent grandmother. Darton &
Harvey, 1804.
A set of cards.

Putsey, W.
JUVENILE CLASS BOOK ; or sequel to the 'Child's
Companion'. Longman, 1818.

Pycroft, James.
COURSE OF ENGLISH READING, adapted to every
taste and capacity. Longman, 1844.
RATIONAL READING LESSONS AND KEY. Simpkin.
(Lond. Cat.).

Raikes, R.
THE SUNDAY SCHOOL SCHOLAR'S COMPANION.
1794.

Ransome, R.
THE ASSEMBLED ALPHABET; or acceptance of A's
invitation . . . . Being a sequel to 'The Invited Alphabet'.
Tabart, 1809. Darton, 1813.
INFANTILE ERUDITION; concluding with a glee for
three voices; to which are added The Figure Dancers. The
whole intended as a supplement to the 'Invited' and
'Assembled' Alphabets.
In William Darton's list in 1820's.
THE INVITED ALPHABET, or address of A to B, con-
taining his friendly proposal for the amusement and inst-
ruction of good children. Darton, 1808. Tabart, 1809.
Darton, 1809.
With twenty-six engraved plates of the letters of the alph-
bet, who are invited to assemble so that children may learn
to read.

THE RATIONAL PRIMER. Darton, 1816.
Illustrated alphabet and first reader.

READING MADE EASY BY MEANS OF THE PHONE-
TIC ALPHABET. London, Bath, 1856.

READING MADE EASY; in a regular and speedy method
of teaching young children to spell and read English.
Dublin, Fox, 1811.

READING MADE QUITE EASY AND DIVERTING.
1746. Edinburgh, W. Coke, 1806.

THE REAL READING MADE EASY. Newcastle, T. Saint,
1782.
A simplified spelling system. Imitates Hastie's 'Only
Method'. Cuts by Bewick.

THE RHYMING ALPHABET. Harvey & Darton, (c.1840).
Coloured plates.

Richardson, Thomas.
NEW ROYAL SPELLING PRIMER. Derby, Richardson,
1835.
RICHARDSON'S BRITISH PRIMER. Derby, Richardson, (c.1825).
RICHARDSON'S CHILD INSTRUCTOR; or, an introduction to the spelling book. Derby, Richardson, (c.1825).

RICHARDSON'S JUVENILE CABINET. Derby, Richardson, (c.1820).
Contains alphabets, including A Apple-Pie.
RICHARDSON'S NEW BATTLEDORE. Derby, (c.1830)
RICHARDSON'S NEW JUVENILE READER, or, a collection of useful, religious, moral and entertaining lessons, in prose and verse, for the use of children. Derby, T. Richardson & Son, 1843.
RICHARDSON'S NEW PRIMER, Derby, Richardson, (c.1825).
RICHARDSON'S NEW ROYAL BATTLEDORE. Derby, Richardson, (c.1830).
Three battledores with varying texts are know with this title.
RICHARDSON'S SUNDAY-SCHOOL READING PRIMER. Derby. Richardson, (c.1845).

Ritson, Mrs. Ann.
THE MONTHLY MONITOR; consisting of easy reading lessons; or, short stories, adapted to every season of the year. Harris & Son, 1821.

THE ROAD TO LEARNING; or, original lessons, in words of one and two syllables, for little children. Harvey & Darton, (c.1844).

(Robson, Mary).
STORIES FOR CHILDREN; chiefly confined to words of two syllables; by the author of 'Aunt Mary's Tales'. 1819. 2nd. ed., rev., W. Darton, 1822.

Roe, Richard Baillie.
ENGLISH SPELLING BOOK, etc. Dublin, 1829.

ROSE AND ANN. An easy first book for children. 2nd. ed., Chapman & Hall, 1840.

ROSEWARNE'S ROYAL BATTLEDORE. Belper, (c.1830).
Inner: decorative alphabet and two woodcuts. Outer: four woodcuts with captions.

Rowbotham, James.
A NEW DERIVATIVE SPELLING-BOOK. Harvey & Darton, (c.1840).

THE ROYAL ABC. Dean & Munday, (c.1835).

THE ROYAL ALPHABET OF KINGS AND QUEENS. Joseph Cundall, 1841.
Hailes Juvenile Library.

ROYAL ALPHABET, or the child's first step to learning. Dundee, Brown, (c.1830).

THE ROYAL ALPHABET OR HISTORY OF AN APPLE PIE. Hodgson & Co., 1822.

ROYAL BATTLEDORE. Otley, W. Walker, (c.1830).

THE ROYAL BATTLEDORE; being the first introductory part of the Circle of the Sciences. Newbery, 1745. Later became:
THE ROYAL BATTLEDORE; or, first book for children. *Various editions, Newbery, Carnan and Collins, 1770-1787. Collins listed Royal Battledore in 1750 as own invention.*

THE ROYAL LONDON PRIMER; or, reading made easy. Johnson (c.1830).

THE ROYAL PRIMER; or, an easy and pleasant guide to the art of reading. 2nd. ed., London, for J. Newbery and B. Collins at Salisbury, 1751. New ed., Hodges & Collins, 1753.
Influenced by the New England Primer. Popular still in the nineteenth century.

THE ROYAL PRIMER, or the first book for children, adapted to their tender capacities. Authorised by His Majesty, King George III. Dublin. Willian Jones, 1818.

THE ROYAL PRIMER OR HIGH ROAD TO LEARNING. J. Harris, 1835.

Rusher, J. G.
THE ENGLISH SPELLING BOOK IMPROVED . . . . 2nd. ed., Banbury, J. G. Rusher, (c.1831).

Rusher, William.
READING MADE MOST EASY; consisting of a variety of useful lessons . . . . 2nd. ed., Banbury, W. Rusher, 1786. 405th. ed., (c.1840).

RUSHER'S ENGLISH PRIMER, or child's first book. Banbury, J. G. Rusher, (c.1829).

RUSHER'S ROYAL PRIMER, IMPROVED. Banbury, J. G. Rusher, (c.1829).

SAEL'S INTRODUCTION TO READING. (2 vols.). W. Walker. (Lond. Cat.).

THE SALISBURY SPELLING-BOOK, with historical and moral extracts from the New Testament . . . . published for the use of Sunday Schools. (1786). 12th. ed., Salisbury, Easton, 1809.

Scottish Schoolbook Association.
   READING LESSON BOOKS:
      THE CHILD'S FIRST BOOK.
      No. 1, PRIMER. (c.1845). Imp. ed., Edinburgh, 1846.
      No. 2, SECOND LESSONS. 1845. Imp. ed., 1846.
      No. 3, THIRD LESSONS. Edinburgh, (c.1845).
      MANUAL OF ENGLISH PRONUNCIATION
      SHEET LESSONS.
      No. 4, READINGS IN PROSE AND VERSE. 1847.
   These are listed in the Committee of Council schedules of 1847.

THE SCRIPTURE ALPHABET. By a parent for his children. Darton, 1811.

THE SCRIPTURE ALPHABET FOR CHILDREN. R.T.S., (c.1820).

A SET OF COLOURED FLOWERS AND THE ALPHABET FOR LITTLE CHILDREN. Darton & Harvey, 1800.

SHORT STORIES, IN WORDS OF ONE SYLLABLE; by the author of 'Summer Rambles'. Lloyd, 1801.

THE SILVER PENNY, for the amusement and instruction of good children. York. Kendrew, (c.1815).
   A chapbook: Picture alphabet and one cut.

THE SILVER PRIMER; or, first book for children. York, Kendrew, 1820. 1834.
   A pictorial alphabet and first reader.

THE SILVER TOY, or, picture alphabet for the entertainment and instruction of children in the nursery. Wellington, Houlston & Son, (c.1825).

SIMPLE STORIES. A very easy reading book. Harvey & Darton, (c.1840).
   With coloured plates.

SIX STORIES FOR THE NURSERY; in words of one or two syllables. By a mother. Godwin, 1819.

Sketch, Sally (Pseud.).
AN ALPHABETICAL ARRANGEMENT OF
ANIMALS FOR LITTLE NATURALISTS. Harris &
Son, 1821.
With twenty-six coloured plates.

Slack, Mrs. Ann(e) (Fisher).
THE NEW ENGLISH TUTOR, or modern preceptor.
(c.1780). 18th. ed., enl. and imp., Newcastle, S. Hodgson,
1821.
NEW ENGLISH EXERCISE BOOK, calculated to
render the construction of the English tongue easy and
familiar, independent of any other language. Newcastle,
Thos. Slack, 1770.
THE PLEASING INSTRUCTOR OR ENTERTAINING
MORALIST, consisting of select essays, relations,
visions and allegories from the most eminent English
authors. . . . 1756. 3rd. ed., 1760. 7th. ed., 1768. Robinson
& Roberts, 1770. New ed., 1777. Newcastle , Robinson &
Hodgson, 1785, 1787. T. Fisher, (c.1786). For the book-
sellers, 1792. Gainsborough, Mozley, 1809. New ed., 1820.
Very popular; often pirated.

Smith, John.
A KEY TO READING. Liverpool, E. & J. Smith, (c.1830).
LESSONS ON WORDS AND OBJECTS. Simpkin &
Marshall, 1834. New ed., 1840.

Smith, Thomas.
AN EASY SPELLING BOOK, for children, beginning
with short lessons in words of one syllable, and proceeding
to those of two, three, or more syllables with a familiar
dialogue between a father and his child. 16th. ed., Derby,
John Drewry, 1790. First part of book only; Nottingham,
H. Barnett, 1816.

Somerville, Elizabeth.
LESSONS FOR CHILDREN OF THREE YEARS OLD.
J. Vigevena, for Crosby & Co., and B. Tabart, (c.1802).
*Also known as SOMERVILLE'S FIRST LESSONS FOR
CHILDREN OF THREE YEARS OF AGE, CONSIS-
TING OF WORDS OF ONE SYLLABLE.*
LESSONS; or, dialogues and stories in two and three
syllables. Sampson, Low, 1801.
LESSONS; or, short stories in two or three syllables. J.
Vigevena for Crosby & Co., and B. Tabart, (c.1802).

SOUTER'S FIRST SCHOOL READER; comprising a selection of reading lessons, progressively arranged. Souter &
Law, 1845.

SOUTER'S FIRST SCHOOL SPELLING AND READING
BOOK. Law, (c.1845).

SOUTER'S PROGRESSIVE PRIMER. A first book for
children. Law, (c.1850).

SOUTER'S SECOND SCHOOL READER. Souter & Law,
1845.

S.P.C.K.
A LITTLE READING BOOK FOR YOUNG
CHILDREN. (c.1825).
EDUCATIONAL SERIES:
THE FIRST BOOK.
THE SECOND BOOK.
THE THIRD BOOK. 1844.
READING SERIES:
No. 1.
No. 2. 1844.
*The educational series and the reading series are listed in
the Committee of Council schedules of 1847.*

THE SPELLING BEE. A letters-try game. (c.1850).
An early version of 'Lexicon'.

SPELLING BOOK AND DICTIONARY OF WORDS IN
COMMON USE. Simpkin. (Lond. Cat.).

A SPELLING DICTIONARY ON A PLAN ENTIRELY
NEW. Newbery, 1745.
*Vol. 3 of the Circle of the Sciences. Later issued separately
as AN EASY SPELLING DICTIONARY ON A NEW
PLAN. Also; SPELLING DICTIONARY OF THE
ENGLISH LANGUAGE ON A NEW PLAN. 7th. ed.,
1760.*

SPELLING, QUESTIONS AND STORIES FOR INFANT
SCHOOLS, AND NURSERIES. Exeter, 1825.

SPRING FLOWERS AND MONTHLY MONITOR, or
early lessons adapted to every season of the year. J.
Harris, 1832.

Steill, Benjamin.
PICTORIAL SPELLING BOOK. A. Hall. (Lond. Cat.).

THE STEP BY STEP SPELLING BOOK. Otley, Walker,
(c.1840).

STEPPING STONES FOR TOTTERING FEET, or reading
lessons adapted to Mrs. Williams' syllabic method.
Hatchard & Co., 1831.

THE STORY OF LITTLE MARY AND HER CAT, in
words not exceeding two syllables. Darton & Clark, 1830.

Sullivan, Robert.
THE SPELLING BOOK SUPERSEDED; or, a new and
easy method of teaching the spelling, meaning, pronuncia-
tion, and etymology of all the difficult words in the
English language. Longman, (c.1845). 123rd. ed., Dublin,
M. & J. Sullivan; London, Longman, etc., (no date).

Sunday School Union.
READING BOOK, Part 1. 1830.
SPELLING BOOK, published for the use of Sunday
Schools. Part 4. Davis & Hamilton, (c.1845).

Tabart, Benjamin.
THE NATIONAL SPELLING BOOK; or, a sure guide to
English spelling and pronunciation arranged on such a
plan as cannot fail to remove the difficulties and facilitate
general improvement in the English language. New ed.,
rev. and corr. by Rev. T. Clark; John Souter, (c.1820).

Taylor, Jane and Gilbert, Ann (Taylor).
LIMED TWIGS, TO CATCH YOUNG BIRDS. (1808).
2nd. ed., Darton, Harvey & Darton, 1811. 7th. ed., Harvey
& Darton, 1828.
Progressive reading lessons in dialogue form.

THE TEACHING PARROT FOR CHILDREN. Darton &
Harvey, 1802.
Contains picture alphabet.

Teachwell, Mrs.
See Fenn, Lady E.

THOMAS LOVECHILD'S ONLY METHOD TO MAKE READING EASY, or, little masters' and misses' best instructor. York, Wilson, 1803.
Cuts by Bewick.

TOM THUMB'S ALPHABET, or new ABC. J. Fairburn, (c.1840).

TOM THUMB'S PLAYBOOK. York, (c.1800).
Contains A was an Archer.

TOM THUMB'S PLAYBOOK. Intended to facilitate the progress of the rising generation in the stence (sic) of A, B, C. Edinburgh, G. Ross, 1814.
Includes A a apple-pye and A was an Angler.

TOM THUMB'S PLAY-BOOK, to teach children their letters as soon as they can speak. Edinburgh, A. Robertson, (c.1760).
Contains A Apple Pye, A was an Archer, catechism, prayers.

TOM THUMB'S PLAY-BOOK; to teach children their letters, by a new and pleasant method. New and improved edn. Alnwick, W. Davison, (c.1830).
Various alphabets, syllables, short words and sentences. Bewick engravings illustrate a few paragraphs.

TOM THUMB'S PLAY-BOOK. Newcastle, Angus for T. Bell, 1824.

THE TRAGICAL DEATH OF A APPLE-PIE. No publisher or date, (c.1830).

THE TRAGICAL DEATH OF A, APPLE-PYE, who was cut in pieces and eat by twenty-five gentlemen with whom all little people ought to be acquainted. Dicey, (18th. C.). Evans, (c.1791). Dean & Munday, (c.1822). Catnach, (c.1825). Batchelor, (c.1830).

THE TRAGICAL DEATH OF A APPLE-PYE, Who was cut in pieces and eaten by twenty-five gentlemen with whom little people ought to be very well acquainted. J. Evans, (c.1820).

THE TRAGICAL DEATH OF AN APPLE PIE. Bishop & Co. (c.1840).

THE TRAGICAL DEATH OF AN APPLE PIE. R. Carr, (c.1840).

THE TRAGICAL DEATH OF AN APPLE PIE. J. Rosewarne, (c.1835).

Trimmer, Mrs. Sarah (Kirby).
THE CHARITY SCHOOL SPELLING BOOK. 1st. ed.,
(THE LITTLE SPELLING BOOK), 1786. Part 1; 4th.
ed., 1798. 5th. ed., 1799. 6th. ed., 1800. 10th. ed., 1807.
New ed., Rivington, 1818. Part 2; 1788. 2nd. ed., 1794. 5th.
ed., Rivington, 1800. New ed., Rivington, 1818. 1823.
EASY LESSONS FOR YOUNG CHILDREN. (c.1787).
3rd. ed., Johnson, 1792. 6th. ed., Johnson, 1807.
EASY LESSONS; or, leading strings to knowledge. New
ed., Grant & Griffith, (c.1850).
THE LITTLE SPELLING BOOK FOR YOUNG CHILD-
REN. 7th. ed., Johnson & Hatchard, 1800.
THE LADDER TO LEARNING. . . . Edited and impro-
ved by Mrs. Trimmer. 16th. ed., Harris, 1841. 17th. ed.,
Grant & Griffith, 1845.
John Newbery's book, bowdlerized.

Turner, Elizabeth.
THE DAISY; or cautionary stories in verse. Adapted to
the ideas of children from four to eight years old. Harris,
1807. J. Harris & Son, 1820.

UNION BATTLEDORE. Alnwick, Davison, (c.1820).
*Three alphabets, numerals, list of words. Bewick
engravings.*

THE UNIVERSAL PRIMER; or a new and easy guide to
the art of spelling and reading. Marshall, (c.1785).

THE UNIVERSAL PRIMER, or reading made easy. W. S.
Johnson, (c.1845).

THE UNIVERSAL PRIMMER; or, child's first lesson.
Congleton, Dean, (c.1810).
*The spelling of the title may indicate a different pronuncia-
tion of the word Primer.*

Vyse, Charles.
THE NEW LONDON SPELLING BOOK; or, the young
gentleman and lady's guide to the English tongue; containing such a variety of really useful matter, as to enable
teachers to instruct their scholars to spell and read the
English language with propriety, without the assistance of
any other book. In which great care has been taken to collect what may teach youth their duty and behaviour towards God and Man, and to avoid the numerous temptations of life, and of their own ungovernable passions. 1777.
1781. 10th. ed., 1791. 11th. ed., 1793. New ed., imp., alt.,
with addns., G. & J. Robinson, 1805. New ed., with imp.
and addns., for G. Wilkie and J. Robinson, etc., 1807.
Robinson, 1809. Dean & Munday, 1813, 1818. Derby,
Mozley, 1824. New ed., London, Hurst, Chance & Co.,
Derby, Richardson, (c.1825). Belper, Rosewarne, (c.1830).
Aberystwith, Williams & Son, (c.1841). McDonald, 1841.
Ryle & Co., 1845. Oxford, Slatten, 1845. Routledge,
(c.1858). Listed by Milner, (c.1860).
Very popular, at least with parents and teachers.

Walker, Donald.
READING AND WRITING, or an improved spelling
book, etc. 1836. New ed., imp., Devonport, 1842.

Wall, Charles.
GRAMMATICAL SPELLING BOOK. Orr. (Lond. Cat.).

WALLIS'S REVOLTING ALPHABET. Wallis, (c.1830).
*Picture of a man with child on his knee; man points to
round mirror on wall; letters appear in mirror when knob
at back is turned.*

Watts, Isaac.
READING MADE EASY. Kendal, M. & R. Branthwaite,
(c.1810).

THE WAY TO READING MADE EASY, or the child's
first book, consisting of Scripture sentences and other
pieces, etc. New ed., Birmingham, Knott & Lloyd, 1811.

W. BELCH'S NEW AND AMUSING ALPHABET (c.1815).

Wesley, John.
LESSONS FOR CHILDREN. 3rd. ed., 1745.
Still in print in nineteenth century.

Wilby, F.
THE INFANT SCHOOL SPELLING-BOOK. Darton & Clark, 1844.

Williams, Helen Maria.
A SUMMARY METHOD OF TEACHING CHILDREN TO READ; upon the principle originally discovered by the Sieur Berthaud. 1817. 5th. ed., Whittaker, etc., 1830. Cheap ed., 1819. Also known as:
SYLLABIC SPELLING; or, a summary method of teaching children to read.
An early attempt at a phonic method; an adaption to English of a French book which had been published forty years earlier, Quadrilles des Enfants.

Wilson, J.
THE YOUTH'S READER; or, second book for children. 2nd. ed., Nottingham, 1822.

Wilson, Lucy.
FANNY AND HER MAMMA, or easy reading lessons. Grant & Griffith, 1848.

Wilson, Rev. William Carus.
CHILD'S FIRST TALES, in words of one syllable. For the use of infant schools and little children in general. (2 vols in 1). Kirby Lonsdale, A. Foster; London, L. & G. Seeley, 1836.

Windett, J.
WINDETT'S IMPERIAL PRIMER, No. 1, etc. (c.1834).

WOOD'S PRETTY ALPHABET FOR CHILDREN. J. T. Wood, (c.1840).

Woodward, Robert William.
NEW ENGLISH SPELLING-BOOK, on an improved plan. 10th. ed., J. Fairburn, (c.1830).

Young, Maria.
THE LITTLE CHILD'S READER, containing original stories adapted to the understanding of young children. Derby, Mozley, (c.1835).

THE YOUNG CHILD'S PRIMER. Bishop & Co., (c.1830).
A chapbook.

YOUTH'S BATTLEDORE. Alnwick, W. Davison, (c.1820).
With three woodcuts.

THE YOUTH'S BEST FRIEND; or reading no longer a task. Deal, Hayward, 1825.

YOUTH'S GUIDE, adapted to the use of schools by a gentleman. Deal, Hayward, 1829.
With illustrated alphabet.

TITLE INDEX

THE BRITISH CHILD'S SPELLING BOOK. Innes, H.
BRITISH CLASS BOOK. Bentley, H.
BRITISH YOUTH'S READER. Innes, H.
BROWN'S ROYAL VICTORIA PRIMER.

CHAMBER'S EDUCATIONAL COURSE.
THE CHARITY SCHOOL SPELLING BOOK. Trimmer, Mrs. S.
THE CHILD'S ALPHABET.
THE CHILD'S ASSISTANT. Hartland, W.
THE CHILD'S BATTLEDORE.
THE CHILD'S BEST INSTRUCTOR IN SPELLING AND READING. . . . Entick, J.
THE CHILD'S FIRST BOOK.
THE CHILD'S FIRST BOOK AND SUNDAY SCHOOL PRIMER.
THE CHILD'S FIRST BOOK; being an introduction to spelling and reading.
THE CHILD'S FIRST BOOK, containing the ABC.
THE CHILD'S FIRST BOOK; containing the alphabet.
THE CHILD'S FIRST BOOK; or, key to reading.
THE CHILD'S FIRST BOOK; or, reading and spelling made easy.
THE CHILD'S FIRST BOOK IMPROVED. . . .
THE CHILD'S FIRST LESSON BOOK.
THE CHILD'S FIRST STEP TO LEARNING.
CHILD'S FIRST STEP UP THE LADDER OF LEARNING.
CHILD'S FIRST TALES. . . . Wilson, W. C.
THE CHILD'S FRIEND.
THE CHILD'S INSTRUCTOR. . . .
THE CHILD'S INSTRUCTOR; or, picture alphabet.
THE CHILD'S MONITOR. . . . Hornsey, J.
THE CHILD'S NEW BOOK OF EASY TALES . . . . Bishop, J.
THE CHILD'S NEW PLAY-THING. . . .
THE CHILD'S NEW SPELLING PRIMER.
THE CHILD'S OWN BATTLEDOOR.
THE CHILD'S PICTURE ALPHABET.
CHILD'S PICTURE READING BOOK.
THE CHILD'S PRIMER.
THE CHILD'S SECOND BOOK.
THE CHILD'S TREASURY OF KNOWLEDGE AND AMUSEMENT. Clark, S.
CHIT CHAT. . . . Budden, M. E.

CLARK'S ENGLISH PRIMER. (Galt, J.).
THE CLASS BOOK. . . . by Rev. D. Blair. (Phillips, Sir R.).
CLASSICAL LETTERS, or alphabet of memory.
CLASSIFIED SPELLING BOOK.
COBBETT'S ENGLISH SPELLING BOOK. Cobbett, W.
COBWEBS TO CATCH FLIES. Fenn, Lady E.
COMICAL HOTCH-POTCH.
COMIC ALPHABET. Cruikshank, G.
COMPREHENSIVE PRIMER. Crossley, J. T.
COMPREHENSIVE READER. Crossley, J. T.
COMPREHENSIVE SPELLING. Crossley, J. T.
COTTAGE LESSONS.
A COURSE OF ELEMENTARY READING. . . .
    M'Culloch, J.
COURSE OF ENGLISH READING. Pycroft, J.
THE CRITICAL SPELLING BOOK. Lowe, S.
CROSSLEY'S SEQUEL. Crossley, J. T.

DAILY LESSON BOOKS.
THE DAISY; or, cautionary stories. . . . (Turner, E.)
DARTON'S SCRIPTURE ALPHABET.
DERIVATIVE SPELLING BOOK. Eves, C.
DIALOGUES CONSISTING OF WORDS OF ONE
    SYLLABLE. . . .
DILSWORTH IMPROVED. James, S.
DIRECTIONS TO PLAY THE LITERARY CARDS. . . .
    Manson, D.

THE EAR AND THE EYE. Marks, E. N.
EARLY LESSONS. Edgeworth, M.
EARLY SEEDS TO PRODUCE SPRING FLOWERS.
    Elliot, M.
AN EARLY STAGE ON THE ROAD TO LEARNING.
THE EASTER GIFT.
AN EASY INTRODUCTION TO THE ENGLISH
    LANGUAGE.
EASY LESSONS FOR YOUNG CHILDREN. Trimmer,
    Mrs. S.
EASY LESSONS, or leading strings to knowledge.
EASY READING. . . . Fenn, E.
AN EASY SPELLING BOOK. Smith, T.
AN EASY SPELLING DICTIONARY.
AN EASY SPELLING DICTIONARY ON A NEW PLAN.
    See A SPELLING DICTIONARY ON A PLAN
    ENTIRELY NEW.

EASY STORIES FOR THE AMUSEMENT AND
  INFORMATION OF CHILDREN. . . .
EDINBURGH ALPHABET.
ELEMENTS OF SPELLING AND READING. Cobbin, I.
THE ENGLISH BATTLEDORE.
THE ENGLISH EXPOSITOR. Duncan, Rev. J.
THE ENGLISH INSTRUCTOR. Dixon, H.
THE ENGLISH PRIMER, or child's first book.
ENGLISH READER. Murray, L.
ENGLISH RURAL SPELLING BOOK. Johnson, C. W.
ENGLISH SPELLING. Graham, G. F.
ENGLISH SPELLING BOOK. Abbott, G. D.
ENGLISH SPELLING BOOK. Hort, W. J.
AN ENGLISH SPELLING BOOK. Masson, A.
THE ENGLISH SPELLING BOOK. Mavor, W. F.
AN ENGLISH SPELLING BOOK. Murray, L.
ENGLISH SPELLING BOOK. Roe, R.
THE ENGLISH SPELLING BOOK AND EXPOSITOR.
  Boad, H.
THE ENGLISH SPELLING BOOK IMPROVED.
  Rusher, J. G.
AN ENGLISH VOCABULARY. Carpenter, T.
ENGLISH VOCABULARY, or spelling book.
THE ENIGMATICAL ALPHABET.
ETYMOLOGICAL SPELLING BOOK AND EXPOSITOR.
  Butter, H.
THE EXCITEMENT. . . . Keys, A.
THE EXPEDITIOUS SELF-INSTRUCTOR. Greig, J.
THE EXPLANATORY ENGLISH SPELLING BOOK.
  Pinnock, W.

FABLES IN MONOSYLLABLES. Fenn, Lady E.
THE FAMILY TESTAMENT. Brown, J.
FANNY AND HER MAMMA. Wilson, L.
THE FEMALE MENTOR. Platts, Rev. J.
FIRST BOOK, FOR CHILDREN. Murray, L.
FIRST ENGLISH READER. Abbott, G. D.
FIRST GUIDE TO READING. Hornsey, J.
THE FIRST LESSON BOOK.
A FIRST, OR MOTHER'S DICTIONARY. Jameson, A. B.
FIRST PHONIC READING BOOK.
THE FIRST SPELLING BOOK FOR CHILDREN.
THE FIRST STEP TO KNOWLEDGE, by Rev. J. Gold-
  smith. Phillips, Sir R.
THE FIRST STEP TO LEARNING.

FISHER'S SPELLING BOOK.
FLORA'S ALPHABET.
THE FRIEND OF MOTHERS. See THE ART OF
   TEACHING IN SPORT.
THE FUNNY ALPHABET.

GAFFER GOODMAN'S PICTURE HORN-BOOKS.
THE GALLOPING GUIDE TO THE ABC.
A GENERAL VIEW OF ENGLISH PRONUNCIATION.
THE GOLDEN ABC.
THE GOLDEN PRIMER.
GOOD AND BAD.
THE GOOD CHILD'S DELIGHT.
THE GOOD CHILD'S DELIGHT. Kilner, J.
THE GOOD CHILD'S REWARD.
A GOOD LITTLE CHILD'S FIRST ABC.
GRADATIONAL SPELLING BOOK. Fellows, J.
GRADED PRIMER. Butter, H.
GRAMMATICAL AND PRONOUNCING SPELLING
   BOOK. Cobbin, I.
GRAMMATICAL SPELLING BOOK. Wall, C.
GRANDMAMMA EASY'S ALDERMAN'S FEAST.
GRANDMAMMA EASY'S NEW STORY ABOUT
   LITTLE JACK HORNER.
GRANDPAPA EASY'S PRETTY POETICAL SPELLING
   BOOK.
GREEN'S FIRST TALES FOR LITTLE CHILDREN.
GREEN'S NURSERY LEADING STRINGS.
GREEN'S UNIVERSAL PRIMER.
A GUIDE TO THE ENGLISH TONGUE. . . . Dyche, T.
GUY'S NEW BRITISH SPELLING BOOK. Guy, J.
GUY'S NEW EXERCISES IN ORTHOGRAPHY. Guy, J.

HARLEQUIN'S ABC.
HARRISON'S JUVENILE INSTRUCTOR. . . .
HARRY'S LADDER TO LEARNING.
HELP FOR INFANTS IN SPELLING, etc. Lloyd, W. F.
THE HISTORICAL ALPHABET.
THE HISTORY OF A APPLE PIE.
THE HISTORY OF AN APPLE PIE.
THE HISTORY OF THE APPLE PIE, WRITTEN BY Z.
THE HISTORY OF LITTLE MARY AND HER DOLL
   JANE. . . .
THE HOUSE THAT JACK BUILT.
HOWE'S PRIMER.
HUMPTY DUMPTY'S GOLDEN ABC.

THE ILLUSTRATED ABC....
THE ILLUSTRATED LONDON SPELLING BOOK.
THE IMPERIAL ALPHABET.
THE IMPERIAL BATTLEDOOR.
THE IMPERIAL BATTLEDORE.
THE IMPERIAL SPELLING BOOK. Bolton. C.
IMPROVED UNIVERSAL SPELLING BOOK. Fenning. D
THE INDESTRUCTABLE ALPHABET.
THE INDESTRUCTABLE READING BOOK.
THE INDESTRUCTABLE SPELLING BOOK.
INFANTILE ERUDITION. Ransome, R.
INFANTINE KNOWLEDGE.
INFANTINE KNOWLEDGE.... Fenn, E.
INFANTINE STORIES .... Fenwick, E.
THE INFANT'S ALPHABET.
THE INFANT'S BATTLEDORE.
THE INFANT SCHOOL SPELLING BOOK. Wilby, F.
THE INFANT'S FRIEND. Fenn, E.
THE INFANT'S LIBRARY
THE INFANT'S PATH STREWED WITH FLOWERS.
THE INFANT'S PATH STREWN WITH FLOWERS.
THE INFANT'S PRIMER.
THE INFANT'S TOY BOOK.
THE INFANT'S TOY BOOK OF PRETTY TALES.
THE INFANT'S TUTOR.
THE INFANT TUTOR, or an easy spelling book. See AN
   EASY INTRODUCTION TO THE ENGLISH
   LANGUAGE.
INNE'S BRITISH MINERVA PRIMER. Innes, H.
INSTRUCTION AND AMUSEMENT UNITED....
INSTRUCTIVE READER. Cobbin, I.
THE INSTRUCTOR.... Fisher, G.
AN INTRODUCTION TO READING AND SPELLING.
   Hewlett, J.
INTRODUCTION TO SPELLING.
AN INTRODUCTION TO SPELLING AND READING.
   Fox, F.
AN INTRODUCTION TO SPELLING AND READING.
   Markham, W.
AN INTRODUCTION TO THE ENGLISH TONGUE.
   Marshall, C.
INTRODUCTION TO THE EXPLANATORY SPELLING
   BOOK. Pinnock, W.
INTRODUCTORY READING BOOK. Hort, W. J.
THE INVITED ALPHABET.... Ransome, R.

JACK DANDY'S DELIGHT.
JENNY WREN ALPHABET.
JUVENILE CLASS BOOK. Putsey, W.
THE JUVENILE KEEPSAKE.
JUVENILE MANUAL OF READING.
THE JUVENILE RAMBLER.
THE JUVENILE READER. Leitch, N.
JUVENILE STORIES AND DIALOGUES.

KEBLE'S NEW PRIMER. . . . Keble, T. H.
KEBLE'S SECOND BRITISH SPELLING BOOK.
   Keble, T. H.
A KEY TO KNOWLEDGE.
A KEY TO READING. Smith, J.
KEY TO THE BOOK FOR TEACHING CHILDREN TO
   READ. . . . Gall, J.
KING ARTHUR'S ALPHABET.

THE LADDER TO LEARNING. Newbery, J.
THE LADDER TO LEARNING. Trimmer, Mrs. S. (Editor)
THE LADY-BIRD'S LOTTERY.
LEIGHTON'S NEW BATTLEDORE.
LESSONS FOR CHILDREN. . . . Barbauld, Mrs. A. L.
LESSONS FOR CHILDREN. Wesley, J.
LESSONS FOR CHILDREN OF THREE YEARS OLD. . .
   Somerville, E.
LESSONS IN READING FOR CHILDREN. . . .
LESSONS ON COMMON THINGS FOR LITTLE
   CHILDREN.
LESSONS ON WORDS AND OBJECTS. Smith, J.
LESSONS; or, dialogues and stories. Somerville, E.
LESSONS; or short stories. . . . Somerville, E.
THE LIFE AND DEATH OF A, APPLE PIE.
THE LIFE AND DEATH ON AN APPLE-PIE
THE LIFE AND DEATH OF JENNY WREN.
THE LIFE AND HISTORY OF A, APPLE-PIE.
LIMED TWIGS. . . . Taylor, J. and Gilbert, A.
THE LITTLE CHILD'S READER. Young, M.
THE LITTLE CHILD'S TUTOR.
THE LITTLE CHRISTIAN'S SUNDAY ALPHABET.
LITTLE FRANK AND OTHER TALES.
LITTLE JACK'S PRIMER.
LITTLE JANE.
LITTLE LESSONS FOR LITTLE FOLK.
LITTLE LESSONS FOR LITTLE LEARNERS.
   Barwell, L. M.

THE LITTLE LOTTERY BOOK FOR CHILDREN.
LITTLE MARY'S BOOKS FOR CHILDREN.
A LITTLE PRETTY POCKET BOOK. Newbery, J.
THE LITTLE PRIMER.
A LITTLE READING BOOK FOR YOUNG CHILDREN.
    S.P.C.K.
THE LITTLE SPELLING BOOK FOR YOUNG
    CHILDREN. Trimmer, Mrs. S.
LITTLE SPELLING BOOK; or, child's best instructor.
LITTLE STORIES FOR LITTLE FOLKS. . . . Kilner, D.
LITTLE STORIES OF ONE AND TWO SYLLABLES. . . .
LITTLE SUSAN.
THE LITTLE TEACHER. . . .
THE LITTLE VOCABULARY. Fenn, Lady E.
THE LOGOGRAPHIC EMBLEMATICAL ENGLISH
    SPELLING BOOK. Lenoir, P.V.
LONDON BATTLEDORE.
THE LONDON NEW BATTLEDORE.
THE LONDON PRIMER. . . . Pelham, M.

MAJA'S ALPHABET.
MAMA'S GIFT. . . . Meeke, Mrs.
MAMMA'S LESSONS. . . .
MARK'S UNIVERSAL PRIMER.
MARTIN'S NURSERY BATTLEDOOR.
MARTIN'S PICTURE BATTLEDORE. . . .
MARY AND HER CAT.
MAVOR'S EASY SPELLING BOOK. Mavor, W. F.
MAVOR'S FIRST BOOK FOR CHILDREN. Mavor, W. F.
MAVOR'S FIRST SPELLING BOOK. Mavor, W. F.
MAVOR'S NEW LONDON SPELLING BOOK.
    Mavor, W. F.
M'CULLOCH'S READING LESSONS. M'Cullock,
    Rev. J. M.
THE MENTORIAN PRIMER. Pinnock, W.
THE MODERN PICTURE ALPHABET OF
    CURIOSITIES.
MODERN SPELLING BOOK AND EARLY EDUCATOR.
    Eves, C.
THE MONITORIAL CLASS BOOKS. Leitch, N.
THE MONTHLY MONITOR. . . . Ritson, Mrs. A.
THE MORAL INSTRUCTOR. . . . Pickburn, J.
MOTHER MUGGINS AND HER DOG TRAP'S ABC.
THE MOTHER'S FIRST BOOK. Marcet, J.
THE MOTHER'S PRIMER. Cole, Lady M. F. B.

THE MOTHER'S PRIMER, or first book for children
Abbot, A.
MOZLEY'S FIRST BOOK FOR CHILDREN. . . .
MRS. LOVECHILD'S GOLDEN PRESENT. . . . Fenn,
Lady E.
THE MURRAY ALPHABET. . . .
MY FIRST LESSON BOOK TO TEACH ME SPELLING
AND READING.
MY NEW BATTLEDORE.
MY OWN ALPHABET OF HISTORY.

THE NATIONAL READER. (Galt, J.).
NATIONAL SPELLING BOOK. . . . Tabart, B.
THE NEW AND COMPLETE SPELLING DICTIONARY.
Fenning, D.
A NEW AND COMPLETE SPELLING DICTIONARY. . . .
on the plan of the late Mr. Fenning. Free, B. D.
A NEW AND ENTERTAINING ALPHABET. . . .
A NEW AND PLEASING INTRODUCTION TO
READING.
NEW BATTLEDORE.
THE NEW BRITISH EXPOSITOR. Guy, Joseph.
THE NEW BRITISH READER. Guy, J.
A NEW DERIVATIVE SPELLING-BOOK. Rowbotham, J.
NEW ENGLISH EXERCISE BOOK. Slack, Mrs. A.
THE NEW ENGLISH SPELLING BOOK.
NEW ENGLISH SPELLING-BOOK ON AN IMPROVED
PLAN. Woodward, R. W.
THE NEW ENGLISH TUTOR. Slack, Mrs. A.
THE NEW EXPOSITOR. . . .
THE NEWEST READING MADE COMPLETELY EASY.
Davies, T.
THE NEWEST READING MADE EASY. Davies, T.
A NEW GUIDE TO THE ENGLISH TONGUE.
Dilworth, T.
A NEW INVENTED HORN BOOK.
THE NEW JUVENILE READER. Platts, J. W.
THE NEW LONDON ALPHABET. . . .
THE NEW LONDON READING, MADE COMPLETELY
EASY.
THE NEW LONDON READING MADE EASY.
THE NEW LONDON SPELLING BOOK. Vyse, C.
THE NEW LOTTERY BOOK. Bewick, T.
A NEW LOTTERY BOOK ON A PLAN ENTIRELY NEW.
THE NEW ORTHOGRAPHICAL ASSISTANT. . . .
Carpenter, C.

THE NEW PARLOUR SPELLING GAME. . . .
NEW PENNY BATTLEDORE.
A NEW PLAY BOOK FOR CHILDREN.
THE NEW PRECEPTOR. Kay, R.
THE NEW PRIMER.
THE NEW PRONOUNCING AND SPELLING BOOK.
　Bigland, J.
THE NEW READING MADE EASY.
THE NEW RHYMING ALPHABET.
NEW ROYAL BATTLEDORE.
NEW ROYAL SPELLING PRIMER. Richardson, T.
A NEW SEQUEL TO MRS. BARBAULD'S LESSONS.
THE NEW SPEAKER. Mavor, W.
A NEW SPELLING-BOOK. Manson, D.
A NEW SPELLING BOOK OF THE ENGLISH
　LANGUAGE. Moore, J. S.
NEW SPELLING DICTIONARY. Entick, J.
THE NEW UNIVERSAL PRIMER.
THE NOTTINGHAM NEW READING MADE EASY.
No. 7 NEW BATTLEDORE.
NURSERY LEADING STRINGS.
NURSERY READING IN WORDS NOT EXCEEDING
　FOUR LETTERS.

THE OFFICER'S DAUGHTERS. . . .
THE ONLY METHOD TO MAKE READING EASY.
　Hastie, T.
OPEN AND SEE. . . .
THE ORIGINAL READING MADE EASY IMPROVED.
ORTHOGRAPHICAL EXERCISES. . . . Alderson, J.
THE OXFORD SPELLING-BOOK. Jones, E.

PAPA'S GIFT FOR A GOOD CHILD.
THE PARENT'S BEST GIFT.
THE PARLOUR TEACHER.
THE PATENT INDESTRUCTABLE PRIMER.
PATHS OF LEARNING STREWN WITH FLOWERS.
PETER PARLEY'S PRIMER. . . .
PETER PIPER'S PRACTICAL PRINCIPLES. . . .
PETER PRATTLE'S NAVAL ABC.
THE PHONETIC SPELLING BOOK.
THE PHONOGRAPHIC AND PHONOTYPIC
　ALPHABETS.
A PICTORIAL ALPHABET. Osbourne, C.
PICTORIAL PANORAMIC ALPHABET. . . .

PICTORIAL SPELLING BOOK. Steill, B.
THE PICTURE ALPHABET.
THE PICTURE ALPHABET, IN PROSE AND VERSE.
THE PICTURE SHOP FOR GOOD CHILDREN.
PICTURES AND POETRY FOR CHILDREN.
THE PICTURESQUE PRIMER, or first steps up the ladder
    of learning.
THE PICTURESQUE PRIMER; or useful matter. . . .
    Fletcher, Rev. W.
PIGEON PIE ALPHABET.
PINNOCK'S EXPLANATORY ENGLISH READER. . . .
    Pinnock, W.
PINNOCK'S JUVENILE READER. Pinnock, W.
PLAIN THINGS FOR LITTLE FOLKS. Elliot, M.
THE PLAY GRAMMAR.
THE PLEASING INSTRUCTOR.
THE PLEASING INSTRUCTOR, OR ENTERTAINING
    MORALIST. Slack, Mrs. T.
POEMS, PICTURES AND ALPHABET OF VERSES.
THE POSTURE MASTER'S GRAND MUSEUM. . . .
PRACTICAL AND ECONOMICAL READERS. Leitch, N.
PRACTICAL ORTHOGRAPHY. Bearcroft, W.
A PRESENT FROM WINDSOR FOR GOOD BOYS AND
    GIRLS. . . .
PRIMER, or, child's best guide.
THE PRIMMER, CORRECTED AND IMPROVED.
PRINCE ARTHUR'S ALPHABET.
THE PRINCE OF WALES' PRIMER. Mayhew, H.
A PROGRESSIVE SPELLING BOOK.
THE PRONOUNCING EXPOSITOR. Hornsey, J.
PRONOUNCING SPELLING BOOK. Fulton, G.
PRONOUNCING SPELLING BOOK. Maccrea, J.
PRONUNCIATION TAUGHT AS AN AMUSEMENT.

THE RATIONAL ENGLISH EXPOSITOR. Birkin, W.
THE RATIONAL PRIMER.
RATIONAL READING LESSONS. Pycroft, J.
THE RATIONAL SPELLING BOOK. Clarke, John.
READING AND SPELLING IN EASY GRADATIONS.
    Butter, H.
READING AND WRITING. . . . Walker, D.
READING BOOK. Sunday School Union.
READING BOOK, containing useful and pleasing lessons.
    England, Rev.
READING DISENTANGLED. Mortimore, Mrs. F. L.
READING EXERCISES. (Phillips, Sir R.).

READING LESSON BOOKS. Commissioners of National
Education in Ireland.
READING LESSON BOOKS. Scottish Schoolbook
Association.
READING MADE COMPLETELY EASY. . . . Paley, W.
READING MADE EASY. Collyer, J.
READING MADE EASY. Watts, I.
READING MADE EASY, BY MEANS OF THE
PHONETIC ALPHABET.
READING MADE EASY; in a regular and speedy
method. . . .
READING MADE MOST EASY. . . . Rusher, W.
READING MADE PERFECTLY EASY. Fenning, D.
READING MADE QUITE EASY AND DIVERTING.
READING WITHOUT TEARS. Mortimore, Mrs. F. L.
THE REAL READING MADE EASY.
THE RHYMING ALPHABET.
RICHARDSON'S CHILD INSTRUCTOR. Richardson, T.
RICHARDSON'S BRITISH PRIMER. Richardson, T.
RICHARDSON'S JUVENILE CABINET. Richardson, T.
RICHARDSON'S NEW BATTLEDORE. Richardson, T.
RICHARDSON'S NEW JUVENILE READER.
Richardson, T.
RICHARDSON'S NEW PRIMER. Richardson, T.
RICHARDSON'S NEW ROYAL BATTLEDORE.
Richardson, T.
RICHARDSON'S SUNDAY-SCHOOL READING
PRIMER. Richardson, T.
THE ROAD TO LEARNING. . . .
ROSE AND ANN.
ROSEWARNE'S ROYAL BATTLEDORE.
THE ROYAL ABC.
ROYAL ALPHABET.
THE ROYAL ALPHABET OF KINGS AND QUEENS.
THE ROYAL ALPHABET OR HISTORY OF AN APPLE
PIE.
ROYAL BATTLEDORE.
THE ROYAL BATTLEDORE.
THE ROYAL LONDON PRIMER.
THE ROYAL PRIMER; or an easy and pleasant guide to
the art of reading.
THE ROYAL PRIMER, or the first book for children.
THE ROYAL PRIMER OR HIGH ROAD TO LEARNING.
ROYAL VICTORIA SPELLING BOOK. Guy, J.
RUSHER'S ENGLISH PRIMER.
RUSHER'S ROYAL PRIMER IMPROVED.

Books which were used for the Teaching of Reading

SAEL'S INTRODUCTION TO READING.
THE SALISBURY SPELLING BOOK.
THE SCHOLAR'S SPELLING ASSISTANT. Carpenter, T.
THE SCRIPTURE ALPHABET.
SECOND ENGLISH READER. Abbott, G. D.
A SET OF COLOURED FLOWERS. . . .
SHORT STORIES, IN WORDS OF ONE SYLLABLE.
SHORT TALES IN SHORT WORDS. Burden, Mrs.
THE SILVER PENNY.
THE SILVER PRIMER. . . .
THE SILVER TOY. . . .
SIMPLE STORIES. A VERY EASY READING BOOK.
SIX STORIES FOR THE NURSERY.
SOUTER'S FIRST SCHOOL READER.
SOUTER'S FIRST SCHOOL SPELLING & READING
  BOOK.
SOUTER'S PROGRESSIVE PRIMER.
SOUTER'S SECOND SCHOOL READER.
S.P.C.K. EDUCATIONAL SERIES. S.P.C.K.
S.P.C.K. READING SERIES. S.P.C.K.
SPELLING. Mylne, W.
SPELLING AND READING BOOKS. Denham, J. F.
THE SPELLING BEE. . . .
A SPELLING BOOK. Lancaster, J.
SPELLING BOOK, Part 4. Sunday School Union.
SPELLING BOOK AND DICTIONARY OF WORDS. . . .
A SPELLING BOOK DESIGNED TO RENDER. . . . Fenn,
  Lady E.
SPELLING BOOK SUPERSEDED. Sullivan, R.
A SPELLING BOOK, with appropriate lessons in reading.
  Cobbett, W.
A SPELLING BOOK WITH EASY READING LESSONS
  . . . . Fenn, Lady E.
A SPELLING BOOK, ... with stepping-stones. . . .
  Cobbett, W.
A SPELLING DICTIONARY OF THE ENGLISH
  LANGUAGE. See AN EASY SPELLING
  DICTIONARY.
A SPELLING DICTIONARY, ON A PLAN ENTIRELY
  NEW.
SPELLING, QUESTIONS AND STORIES. . . .
SPELLING TURNED ETYMOLOGY. Arnold, T. K.
SPRING FLOWERS AND MONTHLY MONITOR. . . .
THE STEP BY STEP SPELLING BOOK.
STEPPING-STONES FOR TOTTERING FEET.
STORIES FOR CHILDREN. Robson, M.

THE STORY OF LITTLE MARY AND HER CAT.
A SUMMARY METHOD OF TEACHING CHILDREN
   TO READ. Williams, Mrs. H. M.
THE SUNDAY SCHOOL SCHOLAR'S COMPANION.
   Raikes, R.
SYLLABIC SPELLING BOOK. See A SUMMARY
   METHOD OF TEACHING. . . .

TEACHER'S TREASURE. Lamont, Mrs.
THE TEACHING PARROT.
THOMAS LOVECHILD'S ONLY METHOD TO MAKE
   READING EASY.
TOM THUMB'S ALPHABET. . . .
TOM THUMB'S PLAYBOOK.
TOM THUMB'S PLAY-BOOK, to teach children their
   letters. . . .
THE TRAGICAL DEATH OF A APPLE PIE.
THE TRAGICAL DEATH OF A, APPLY-PYE.
THE TRAGICAL DEATH OF AN APPLE PIE.

UNION BATTLEDORE.
UNIVERSAL CLASS BOOK. Maunder, S.
THE UNIVERSAL EXPLANATORY ENGLISH
   READER. . . . Pinnock, W.
THE UNIVERSAL EXPLANATORY SPELLING
   BOOK. . . . Pinnock, W.
THE UNIVERSAL PRIMER.
THE UNIVERSAL PRIMER; or, reading made easy.
THE UNIVERSAL PRIMMER.
THE UNIVERSAL SPELLING BOOK. Fenning, D.

WALLIS'S REVOLVING ALPHABET.
THE WAY TO READING MADE EASY.
W. BELCH'S NEW AND AMUSING ALPHABET.
WINDETT'S IMPERIAL PRIMER. Windett, J.
WOGAN'S IMPROVED SPELLING BOOK. Fenning, D.
WOOD'S PRETTY ALPHABET FOR CHILDREN.

THE YOUNG CHILD'S PRIMER.
THE YOUNG CHRISTIAN INSTRUCTED IN
   READING. Paley, W.
THE YOUNG SCHOLAR'S SPELLING BOOK. Leitch, N.
YOUTH'S BATTLEDORE.
THE YOUTH'S BEST FRIEND.
YOUTH'S GUIDE. . . .
THE YOUTH'S READER. Wilson, J.

APPENDIX B

A LIST OF DATES

Acts, Bills, Reports, educational events, publications, and developments in printing and allied trades.

1797 Bell: *An Experiment in Education*.

1798 Edgeworth: *Practical Education*.
Mechanical paper-making invented.

1799 Religious Tract Society founded.

1800 Lithography patented in England.

1801 General Enclosure Act.
Mavor's *English Spelling Book*.
Plaster - of - Paris method of making stereotypes perfected.

1802 Peel's Health and Morals of Apprentices Act.

1803 Sunday School Union.
Lancaster: *Improvements in Education*.
Fourdrinier brothers and Gamble set up paper-making machines.

1804 Stanhope's iron press.

1805 Mrs. Trimmer: *Comparative View*.
Stereotyping in use at Clarendon Press.

1807 Whitbread's Parochial Schools Bill.

1809 Edgeworth: Essays on Professional Education.

1810 Royal Lancasterian Association founded.
First successful power-driven cylinder press.

1811 National Society founded.

1813 Scott's *Rokeby*: 10,000 in three months. New era in fiction.

1814 Scott's *Waverley* successful.
Koenig's steam press used to print *The Times*.

1815 Select Committee to investigate 'the state of the children employed in the manufactories of the United Kingdom.'
End of war.
Scott's *Guy Mannering*: 2,000 sold a day after publication.

1816 Report on the Education of the lower orders of the Metropolis.
Scott's *The Antiquary*: 6,000 in first six days.
Outburst of radical journalism. Cobbett's *Political Register*.

1817 Albion press invented.

1818 Scott's *Rob Roy*: 10,000 in two weeks.

1819 Peel's Factory Act.

1820 Brougham's Parish Schools Bill.

1821 Scott's *Kenilworth*.
Cobbett's *Sermons*.

1822 Limbird's *Mirror of Literature*: first successful cheap weekly.
Pickering's "Diamond Classics" - large-scale use of cloth bindings.
Church's letter-founding machine.

1823 Wilderspin: *Education of Infant Children of the Poor*.
Swiss Family Robinson.
Catnach's *Murder of Weare*: 250,000. Account of Trial: 500,000.

1824 Combination Laws repealed.
London Infant School Society founded.
Cobbett's *History of the Protestant 'Reformation'* - 40,000 per number.

1825 S.D.U.K. founded.
Brougham: *Practical Observations on the Education of the People* - 20 editions in year.

1827 Cheap 'libraries' begin - Constable's Miscellany and the Library of Useful Knowledge.

1828 Catnach's *Confession and Execution of William Corder*: 1,166,000.

1829 Cadell issues Scott's novels at 5/- a volume.
Murray's 'Family Library' begins.
Stereotyping perfected.

1830 Colburn and Bentley issue reprinted fiction at 6/-.
Henry Butter: *The Etymological Spelling Book*.
Machine binding supersedes hand binding.

1831 'War of unstamped press.'
Chambers' *Edinburgh Journal*.

1832 Reform Act.
First illustrated penny story magazine - *Strange's Penny Story-Teller*.
Penny Magazine and S.P.C.K.'s *Saturday Magazine*.
Steam printing for illustrations.

1833 Roebuck's Education Act. First Education vote - £20,000.
Shaftesbury's Factory Act.
Favell Lee Bevan: *Peep of Day*.
S.D.U.K.'s *Penny Cyclopaedia*.

1834 Report on State of Education by Select Committee reveals deplorable state of schools.

1835 Baxter's experiments in colour printing.

1836 Success of *Pickwick Papers* begins vogue of fiction in shilling parts.
CATNACH'S 'Execution Papers' on Greenacre-Gale murder: 1,650,000.
Newspaper tax reduced to a penny.

1837 Report on the education of the poorer classes.
Paper duty cut by half.
Jacobi's experiments with half-tone blocks.

1838 Kay-Shuttleworth opens Training College at Norwood.
Nicholas Nickleby: first number - 50,000.
Chartist agitation for better educational provision.

1839 Committee of Council for Education established.
First official figures on literacy: males 67%, females 51%.
Catherine Sinclair: *Holiday House*.

1840 Battersea Normal School opened.
Penny Post.
From 1840: Great increase in circulation of weekly newspapers.
Steam printing generally adopted.
Wood-pulp paper introduced.
Photography develops use of lithography.

1842 Mudie's circulating library begins.
Illustrated London News.

1843 Graham's Factory Bill.
Dickens' *Christmas Carol*: 6,000 first day, 15,000 in year.

1844 *The Chimes*: 20,000 'almost at once.'

1845 *The Cricket on the Hearth*: 30,000.

1846 Pupil-Teacher system founded.
Lear's *Book of Nonsense*.

1847 McIntyre & Simm's Parlour Library: reprints for 1/-.
Marryat's *The Children of the New Forest*.

1848 Routledge's Railway Library.
W. H. Smith & Son take lease on bookstall at Euston.
The Haunted Man: 18,000 first day.
Marryat's *Masterman Ready*.
Rotary press invented.

1849 *David Copperfield*: 25,000
5,000,000 broadsides etc. on Jermy and O'Connor murders.

1850 W.J.Fox's Education Bill.
Ewart's Public Libraries Bill enacted.
House-hold Words begins at 100,000.

BIBLIOGRAPHY

Altick, Richard D. *The English Common Reader*. University of Chicago Press, 1957.

Ashton, John. *Chap-Books of the Eighteenth Century*. New York: Benjamin Blom, 1967.

Barnard, H.C. *A History of English Education from 1760*. University of London Press, 1961.

Children's Books of Yesterday. A catalogue of an exhibition held at 7 Albermarle Street, during May, 1946. National Book League, 1946.

A Chronical of Boys' and Girls' House. Toronto Public Library, 1964.

Clarke, W.K.Lowther. *A History of the S.P.C.K.* S.P.C.K., 1959.

Cutt, M. Nancy. *Mrs Sherwood and her Books for Children*. Oxford University Press, 1974.

Darton, F.J.Harvey. *Children's Books in England*. Cambridge University Press, 1958.

Dearden, James S. "This printer-inventor almost made history", *Small Printer*, No. 18, June 1966, pp. 13-19.

Diack, Hunter. *In Spite of the Alphabet*. Chatto & Windus, 1965.

Dunn, Henry. *Principles of Teaching*. 14th. ed., Sunday School Union, Hamilton Adams & Co., and Simpkin, Marshall, c.1850.

Early Children's Books: a catalogue of the collection in the London Borough of Hammersmith's Public Libraries. London Borough of Hammersmith, 1965.

Ellis, Alec. *A History of Children's Reading and Literature*. Pergamon Press, 1968.

Fries, Charles C. *Linguistics and Reading*. New York: Holt, Rinehart & Winston, Inc., 1963.

Good, David.(ed.). *A Catalogue of the Spencer Collection of Early Children's Books and Chapbooks*. Harris Public Library, 1967.

Gray, W.S. *The Teaching of Reading and Writing*. Paris: U.N.E.S.C.O., 1956.

Higson, Dr. C.W.J.(ed.). *Sources for the History of Education*. Library Association, 1967.

James, Louis. *Fiction for the Working Man, 1830-1850*. Oxford University Press, 1963.

James, Philip. *Children's Books of Yesterday*. The Studio Ltd., 1933.

Johnson, Clifton. *Old-Time Schools and School-Books*. New York: Dover Publications, Inc., 1963.

Jones, M.G. *The Charity School Movement*. Frank Cass & Co. Ltd., 1964.

Journal of the Statistical Society of London, Vol.1, 1838.

Journal of the Statistical Society of London, Vol.2, Chas. Knight & Co., 1839.

The London Catalogue of Books published in Great Britain, 1816-1851.

Mathews, Mitford M. *Teaching to Read Historically Considered*, University Chicago Press, 1966.

McLean, Ruari. *Pictorial Alphabets*, Studio Vista, 1969.

McLuhan, Marshall. *The Gutenberg Galaxy*. Routledge & Kegan Paul, 1967.

Muir, Percy. *English Children's Books 1600-1900*. Batsford, 1954.

Neuburg, Victor E. *The Penny Histories*. Oxford University Press, 1968.

Newbery, John. *A Little Pretty Pocket-Book*, introduced by M.F.Thwaite. Oxford Univesity Press, 1966.

Quayle, Eric. *The Collector's Book of Children's Books*. Studio Vista, 1971.

Roscoe, S. *Newbery-Carnan-Power*. A provisional check-list... 1966.

St. John, Judith.(ed.). *The Osborne Collection of Early Children's Books, 1566-1910*. Toronto Public Library, 1958.

Sellman, Roger R. *Devon Village Schools in the Nineteenth Century*. Newton Abbot: David & Charles, 1967.

Steinberg, S.H. *Five Hundred Years of Printing*. Penguin, 1965.

Stockham, Peter. *Chapbook ABC's*. Dover, 1974.

Sturt, Mary. *The Education of the People*. Routledge & Kegan Paul, 1967.

Thwaite, M.F. *From Primer to Pleasure*. Library Association, 1963.

Twyman, Michael. *John Soulby, Printer, Ulverston*. University of Reading; Museum of English Rural Life, 1966.

Victorian Children's Books. Victoria & Albert Museum, 1973.

Vries, Leonard de. *Flowers of Delight*. Dobson, 1965.

Webb, R.K. *The British Working Class Reader 1790-1848*. Allen & Unwin, 1955.

Whalley, Joyce I. *Cobwebs to Catch Flies*. Elek, 1974.

Real

Sailor

Collected by John Ashton
Introduced by A. L. Lloyd

Songs

REAL SAILOR SONGS

John Ashton is well known for the quaint and curious studies he produced along the byways of English life and literature, and now this fine book, first issued in 1891 by the Leadenhall Press, is available once again with a fascinating new introduction by A. L. Lloyd.

Strongly bound in an appropriate navy-blue art canvas, and with over two hundred blocks for you to tackle (they cry out to be hand-coloured!) this attractive volume richly deserves a place in any library devoted to folksong, or the sea.

Price: £6 post free

Note: a special edition on cream laid paper, limited to one hundred copies, can also be had—*but directly from the publisher only*—at £6.50 post free.

CURIOSITIES OF STREET LITERATURE

Charles Hindley's strange collection of cocks and catch-pennies, broadsides, squibs and murder ballads first appeared in 1871, and was then re-issued in two thick volumes with an introduction by Leslie Shepard in 1966. Copies of this weird and wonderful reprint—"There has been, and will be, nothing published this year better worth buying and keeping . . ." wrote Anthony Burgess in his generous review in the Sunday Times—are still in stock at the warehouse.

Price: £10 post free

BROADSHEET KING
15 Mortimer Terrace, N.W.5